Contents

Content Guidance

Questions & Answers

Getting the most from this book

Questions & Answers

Exam-style questions

Examiner comments on the questions
Tips on what you need to do to gain full marks, indicated by the icon (e).

Sample student answers
Practise the questions, then look at the student answers that follow each set of questions.

Examiner commentary on sample student answers
Find out how many marks each answer would be awarded in the exam and then read the examiner comments (preceded by the icon (e)) following each student answer. Annotations that link back to points made in the student answers show exactly how and where marks are gained or lost.

Psychology of addictive behaviour (3)   Question **6**

Question 6 **Psychology of addictive behaviour (3)**

(a) Outline the theory of planned behaviour as a model for addiction prevention. (4 marks)

(b) Discuss the effectiveness of types of intervention used to reduce addictive behaviour. (20 marks)

(e) This is a question in parts that requires only descriptive material relating to the theory of planned behaviour as a model for addiction prevention in part (a). It should be noticed that part (a) offers 4 marks, so care should be taken not to overdo the description as it will not gain any extra credit and would waste valuable time better spent on part (b). It should also be remembered there are 4 more AO1 marks available in part (b) for outlining types of intervention, but that the vast majority of the marks available here is for an evaluation, which must focus on the effectiveness of the types of intervention outlined.

Student answer

(a) The theory of planned behaviour arose out of the earlier theory of reasoned action a, but with the addition of a new component, that of the influence of perceived control b. The model comprises several components c: behavioural beliefs, which determine one's attitude towards dependency d, normative beliefs, which concern social pressures to be involved in dependency behaviour e and control beliefs, which determine perceived behavioural control relating to an individual's belief that they can control their dependency behaviour f. If an individual's perceived behavioural control leads them to believe that they can control or quit their addiction g then the model predicts that they will be able to do so. Walsh and White (2007) found support for the theory h, as measurements of TPB constructs were found to accurately predict intentions and actual behaviour. This was further supported i by Oh and Hsu (2001), who found, using a questionnaire, an association between gamblers' attitudes, behavioural intentions and actual behaviour. However, a criticism of the model c is that it presumes behaviour is conscious, reasoned and planned, which may not necessarily always be the case with addicts and the model is also heavily reliant on evidence from self-reports, which may be subject to idealised answers k where addicts give responses according to how they'd like to be rather than how they actually are. In the model's favour, it does have a constructive practical application c, as a treatment process that health practitioners can tailor to individual addicts' needs.

(e) The first part of this answer a explains the TPB generally, b focusing specifically on addiction prevention as the question requires and in some detail, though not sufficiently to merit all 4 marks available. The second part of the answer goes on c to evaluate the theory, which is not required and which therefore is not creditworthy and wastes time that would have been better spent earning credit answering other questions.
AO1 = 3/4

Unit 4 (Sections B & C): Psychology in Action and Research Methods   89

About this book

This guide will help you prepare for the AQA(A) A2 Psychology Unit 4 examination (the psychopathology section is covered in the preceding book in this series) and is intended as a support device for revision and learning. The guide looks first at the specification content and how it is examined, and second at how answers of varying quality are assessed.

Using this guide

You can use this guide in a variety of ways. Each time you start a new topic on your course (e.g. reducing addictive behaviour), use the guide to give you a quick overview of what is involved. Reread each topic at regular intervals as you are studying it in class.

When you start revising, use the unit guide to review the specification areas you have studied (such as belief in exceptional experience), to refresh your learning and to consolidate your knowledge of each of the Unit 4 topics covered.

Content Guidance section

The Content Guidance section explains the specification content for each topic fully so that you understand what is required from you in your examination. Content appropriate to each topic is outlined, to the extent that it would be possible to construct an answer to possible questions set on that topic from the information given. You should note that other content may be equally appropriate.

Of the topics covered in this guide the AQA specification requires you to study the following major areas.

Section B: Psychology in Action

You should study one of the following three contemporary applications of psychology.

Media psychology

- Media influences on social behaviour
- Persuasion, attitude and change
- The psychology of celebrity

The psychology of addictive behaviour

- Models of addictive behaviour
- Vulnerability to addiction
- Reducing addictive behaviour

Anomalistic psychology

- The study of anomalous experience
- Explanations for anomalous experience
- Research into exceptional experience

- It is possible to test evolutionary theory by making predictions based on the theory and then seeing if real-life examples support the predictions. Evolutionary theory is accused of being reductionist as it reduces behaviour down to the single explanation of adaptive fitness, thus ignoring possible other explanations. It is also accused of being deterministic in seeing behaviour as driven by biological factors with no input for free will.

Research into intense fandom

Some individuals form such an interest in celebrities that they can be considered **parasocial** (one-sided) relationships. Such intense fandom can occur at several levels, from a fairly harmless, even quite healthy, form of celebrity worship, to more sinister, intense levels, such as celebrity stalking, defined as 'the wilful, malicious and repeated following or harassing of a celebrity that threatens his or her safety'.

Celebrity worship

fandom the collective supporters of a specific celebrity interest

Examiner tip
The focus here is on research into intense fandom but it should be remembered that the term research does not relate just to research studies but also to explanations of intense fandom and that, therefore, material focused on both these areas would be creditworthy.

Research

- **McCutcheon et al. (2002)** conducted research on 262 participants from Florida and developed the **celebrity attitude scale**, measuring items on three categories of celebrity worship:
  - **entertainment subscale** — measures social aspects of celebrity worship, like discussions with friends
  - **intense-personal subscale** — measures strength of feelings and levels of obsession
  - **borderline-pathological subscale** — measures levels of uncontrollable feelings and behaviour

  It was concluded that celebrity worship has a single dimension, with lower-scoring individuals showing an avid interest in celebrities, such as reading about them, while high-scoring individuals tend to over-identify and become obsessive about celebrities.
- **Maltby et al. (2003)** amassed data from over 1,700 British participants aged between 14 and 62, finding three dimensions of fandom:
  - **entertainment-social** — people who are attracted to celebrities for their entertainment value
  - **intense-personal** — people who develop obsessive tendencies towards celebrities
  - **borderline-pathological** — people who develop uncontrollable fantasies and behaviour patterns
- **Maltby et al. (2004)** found that those in the entertainment-social category were mentally healthy, but those in higher categories were prone to poor mental and physical health.
- **Gabriel (2008)** gave 348 students an 11-item questionnaire measuring self-esteem and they then had to write a short essay about their favourite celebrity, followed by filling in the same questionnaire again. Participants who initially scored low on self-esteem, scored much higher after writing the essay, suggesting that they assimilated the celebrities' characteristics into themselves and thus boosted self-esteem. This was possibly something they could not do in real relationships as fear of rejection stopped them getting close to people.

Section C: Psychological Research and Scientific Method

You should study all the following topics:
- The application of scientific method in psychology
- Designing psychological investigations
- Data analysis and reporting on investigation

The main issues, themes and debates that you need to be familiar with in the study of these A2 Unit 4 topics are covered in this guide. The aim is to give an overview of these topics and to outline the key points you need to know in order to tackle the unit examination. However, you should remember that, for a full and adequate knowledge of the subject matter of this unit, you also need to study your textbook(s) and refer to the notes you make during your course. You can use the points made in this section both to organise your own notes and studies, and as a revision aid when preparing for the examination.

Questions & Answers section

When practising for the examination, use the Questions & Answers section. A sample question for each topic is provided, along with an explanation of its requirements. Sample answers are also provided, accompanied by examiner's comments explaining the strengths and limitations of each answer.

Ideally you should attempt the questions yourself before reading the sample answers and examiner's comments and then compare your answers with the ones given. If you do not have time for this, you should at least make brief plans that you could use as the basis of an answer to each question. Study the sample answer and the examiner's comments and add the key points from them to your own answer or plan.

Content Guidance

In this section, guidance is given on each of the three subsections of the four topics covered by this unit guide. Each subsection starts by providing an outline and explanation of what the specification demands. This is followed by a more detailed examination of the theories, research studies and evaluative points for each subsection.

A general pattern for each topic is followed, wherever appropriate:
- an outline and explanation of the demands of the specification
- a description of the subject matter and relevant research evidence
- evaluative points

It is important to remember that research evidence can be used either as descriptive material (AO1) or as evaluation (AO2/AO3) when answering examination questions. It is advisable to learn how to make use of such material in an evaluative way, for instance by using wording such as 'this supports' or 'this suggests'.

For the research quoted, names of researchers and publication dates are given. Full references for these should be available in textbooks and via the internet if you wish to study them further.

Media psychology

Media influences on social behaviour

Specification content
- *Explanations of media influences on pro- and antisocial behaviour*
- *The positive and negative effects of computers and video games on behaviour*

The specification focuses on explanations of media influences on pro- and antisocial behaviour, as well as the effects video games and computers have on behaviour. There is no direction to concentrate on explicit topic areas and any relevant material would therefore be acceptable in answer to examination questions set.

media influences the effects that public forms of communication have upon pro- and antisocial behaviour

Explanations of media influences on pro- and antisocial behaviour

The term 'media' refers to any form of communication of popular culture, such as television, radio, films, magazines and more modern forms such as computers. There is a long-running argument as to whether media sources exert an influence

on pro- and antisocial behaviour. This is a complex question involving more than the mere imitation of what is viewed. There are many psychological factors to consider and it does appear to be true to say that media influences are on the increase. By 2005 we were watching an average of 2.5 hours each a day of television involving witnessing a high proportion of pro-social and antisocial behaviour. Indeed, the average 16-year-old has witnessed about 13,000 violent television deaths.

Social learning theory

Learning via the media is seen as occurring by **indirect reinforcement**, where an observed behaviour that is reinforced is imitated (**vicarious learning**). Through social learning humans learn the value of specific behaviours and how and when to imitate them.

Bandura (1965) outlined four steps of modelling.
(1) Attention — attention is paid to attractive, high-status and similar models.
(2) Retention — observed behaviours need to be memorised.
(3) Reproduction — imitation occurs only if a person has the skills to reproduce the observed behaviour.
(4) Motivation — direct and indirect reinforcements (both negative and positive) as well as punishments influence the motivation to imitate.

A model is necessary for imitation, but also good levels of **self-efficacy** (situation-specific confidence) are required.

Media influences have formed the basis of much research, and it has been found that if an observer identifies with the perpetrator of a specific act and/or the more realistic or believable the act of aggression is, the more likely imitation becomes. However, if the perpetrator of an act is punished for their behaviour, it decreases the chances of the behaviour being imitated.

SLT also argues that media portrayals of pro-social acts have an equal impact: for instance watching examples of people helping others and being rewarded for it should motivate individuals to imitate such behaviour.

Research

- **Bandura et al. (1961, 1963)** showed children various scenarios involving aggressive behaviour towards an inflatable Bobo doll, finding that they were likely to behave aggressively — and (after being deliberately frustrated) would especially imitate specific behaviours they had observed — when allowed to play with the doll. Bandura concluded that the chances of aggressive acts being imitated increased if the aggressive model was reinforced, but decreased if the model was punished, suggesting that although observational learning can occur, imitation will only be seen if the behaviour is vicariously reinforced. Aggression was also more likely to be imitated if a child identified with the model (for example boys were more aggressive if the model was male and to a lesser extent girls were more aggressive if the model was female) or had low self-esteem.

---

pro-social behaviour actions that are intended to benefit others

antisocial behaviour actions that go against the basic principles of society

social learning the acquisition of pro- and antisocial behaviours through observation and imitation of role models

Examiner tip

When outlining and evaluating theories, such as the SLT, it is important that the theory is explained and evaluated in terms of the topic in focus, for example, media influences on pro- and antisocial behaviour, rather than just outlining and evaluating the theory, as such answers would probably be regarded as no better than basic.

- **Leyens et al. (1975)** divided juvenile delinquents into two groups of aggressive and non-aggressive boys. Half of each group watched violent films and half non-violent films. There was an increase in aggression among those watching violent films, suggesting that social learning was at play rather than personality factors.
- **Charlton (1998)** found no increase in aggressiveness among children on St Helena when television was introduced, though the children came from stable homes and deviant behaviour was practically unknown on the island.
- **Lovelace and Huston (1983)** suggested that learning from pro-social programmes was situation specific and that engaging in discussion with children after watching such programmes, plus related play, enhanced the pro-social effects.
- **Hearold (1986)** found pro-social television affected pro-social behaviour more than antisocial television affected antisocial behaviour, suggesting the power of television in influencing pro-social behaviour is strong.

Evaluation

- Although there is a correlation between the amount of aggressive television watched and the degree of aggressive behaviour, causality is not demonstrated. It may be that aggressive people choose to watch violent programmes.
- Many studies measure only the short-term effects of pro- and antisocial media.
- Huesmann (1988) reports that children use television models to direct their own actions. Observed aggressive acts are stored in memory, where they are strengthened and elaborated through repetition. These memorised acts are then used to guide behaviour in situations perceived as appropriate, suggesting that media influences are a source of social learning.
- Bandura's Bobo doll studies attract many criticisms. Bobo dolls are not real, cannot retaliate and are designed to be hit. As the situation was unfamiliar, children may have acted as they thought they were supposed to do (demand characteristics). There are also ethical concerns over deceit, informed consent, harm and long-term effects on behaviour.
- Many studies do not differentiate between real aggression and play fighting.

Cognitive priming

Cognitive priming involves the presentation of cues in programmes and has been seen to have an effect on aggressive and pro-social behaviour. It is thought that people store in the memory violent and pro-social acts they have seen, as scripts for later behaviour. Being in a similar scenario 'triggers' the script into action.

cognitive priming the presentation of media cues that affect pro- and antisocial behaviour

Research

- **Josephson (1987)** found that boys who watched a violent programme involving communicating via walkie-talkies and then received instructions via a walkie-talkie when playing ice-hockey were more aggressive than those who did not watch the programme.

Examiner tip
To create high-grade evaluative material in answers concerning media influences on pro- and antisocial behaviour it is useful to focus on the potential for practical applications. For example, cognitive priming suggests that media presentations can use cues for pro-social behaviour that will be triggered into action when individuals are in a similar scenario to the media presentation.

- **Murray et al. (2007)** took fMRI brain scans of children watching violent and non-violent films and found those watching violence had active brain areas associated with emotion, arousal and episodic memory, suggesting the storing of aggressive scripts for later use.
- **Moriarty and McCabe (1977)** found that children exposed to media models of sportspeople behaved pro-socially and performed more pro-social acts, suggesting that the programme models acted as cognitive primers for actual behaviour.
- **Holloway et al. (1977)** found participants were more cooperative in bargaining if they heard a pro-social message on the radio first, which implies a pro-social effect from cognitive priming via the media.

Evaluation

- Increased rates of aggression may be due to the high level of violent media acts witnessed, providing violent scripts for actual behaviour.
- Cognitive priming may most affect those with a disposition for aggression or pro-social behaviour.
- Cognitive priming suggests a practical application in developing pro-social behaviours via media sources.

Stereotyping

stereotyping an assumption that everyone in a group of people has the same characteristics and behavioural tendencies

Media sources tend to use **stereotyping** as a quick method of communication. However, these can be non-factual (e.g. the use of British actors to portray baddies in American films, whose roles are often contrived to portray exaggerated negative models).

Research

- **Gunter (1986)** investigated gender role stereotypes and found that those watching most television had more stereotypical beliefs, suggesting that stereotypes do influence behaviour.
- **Dill et al. (2008)** found that men exposed to media stereotypes of sexual harassment became more tolerant of such behaviour. Long-term exposure led to even greater tolerance, suggesting that stereotyping may have a substantial effect on behaviour.

Evaluation

- It may be that people with stereotypical views prefer to watch more television, as it contains stereotypes.
- Media stereotypes may be so exaggerated as to make imitation of them unsustainable in real-life scenarios.
- Stereotyping may be an effective way of coding pro- and antisocial behaviours in the media.

Desensitisation

Desensitisation involves the reduction or elimination of cognitive, emotional and behavioural responses to a stimulus. It is possible that constant exposure to media violence desensitises and makes us 'comfortably numb' to violence in real life. Overexposure to pro-social media similarly reduces its effect, creating 'compassion fatigue' where individuals become numb to pro-social acts and the plight of suffering others.

Research
- **Bushman and Anderson (2007)** found that exposure to violent media produced physiological desensitisation when people later viewed scenes of real violence.
- **Bushman (2009)** found that participants who played violent video games for 20 minutes took longer to respond to someone injured in a staged fight than those viewing non-violent games, suggesting that desensitisation had taken place.
- **Moeller (1999)** reported how donations to media campaigns decreased after a media appeal to help victims of a natural disaster, illustrating the desensitisation effect of compassion fatigue on pro-social behaviour.

Evaluation
- Desensitisation is based on the behavioural technique of systematic desensitisation, lending it theoretical support, but its therapeutic use is indeed systematic, which does not appear to be the case with media output.
- Aretakis and Rameris (2001) believe over-exposure to media violence retards the development of emotion regulation skills, leading to desensitisation to cues that normally trigger empathetic responses, finally leading to aggressive behaviour.

Displacement

People watching a lot of television encounter displacement in thinking that the world is more dangerous than it really is. Factual and news programmes emphasise this danger by focusing on violent stories. Showing antisocial behaviours that actually impinge on daily life much less in reality creates a **deviance amplification effect**, where an increasing cycle of reporting of antisocial behaviours occurs.

Research
- **Gerbner and Gross (1976)** found that frequent viewers of television rated the real world as more dangerous than it really is, supporting the idea of displacement.
- **Cohen (1968)** reported that an absence of news led to an incident of minor affray in Clacton between mods and rockers becoming front-page news. This then developed into a moral panic, supporting the idea of a deviance amplification effect.

desensitisation the lowering of emotional sensitivity by repeated exposure to media influences

displacement the tendency for media to convince people that the world is more dangerous than it really is by overemphasising examples of antisocial discord

In what ways can media influence pro- and antisocial behaviour?

Evaluation

- White (2008) believes that deviance amplification is a media phenomenon that explains inflated concern with knife crime.
- Wilkins (1964) coined the term deviance amplification to explain how the media actually generate an increase in deviancy by making minor and rare problems seem commonplace.

The positive and negative effects of video games and computers on young people

Video games

video games electronic and computerised games played by manipulating visual images

Video games give players a more active role in the experience than other media, often actively encouraging and rewarding violent behaviour within a game. Interest has focused upon whether such behaviour is repeated in real-life scenarios. Children exposed to video games tend to be retarded in their development of emotion-regulation skills, leading to desensitisation to cues normally triggering empathetic responding, which can in turn increase the likelihood of violent behaviour. Desensitisation to violence occurs through repeated exposure to video-game aggression, with emotional desensitisation causing the numbing of emotional reactions to events that should produce a strong response. Cognitive desensitisation occurs when the usual belief that violence is uncommon is replaced with a belief that violence is commonplace and likely. Desensitisation disrupts the process of moral evaluation, causing actions to be taken without consideration for their ethical implications.

Individual, gender and age differences have been identified, as well as a tendency for addictive behaviour. Some research shows game-playing to have positive aspects in its influence on learning and levels of self-esteem, with creative and pro-social games having an educational value and other games releasing stress and aggression in non-harmful ways.

Research

- **Funk et al. (2004)** tested 150 American adolescents, finding that exposure to video-game violence was related to lower empathy and stronger pro-violence attitudes. It was believed that the active nature of playing video games, the intense engagement and the tendency to translate the experience into fantasy play might explain the negative impact.
- **Funk (1995)** found that success at video games came from identifying and choosing violent strategies resulting in a continuous cycle of violence, which was presented as justified, without negative consequences and fun.
- **Strasburger and Wilson (2002)** found that playing video games desensitised the user to the consequences of violence, increased pro-violence attitudes and altered cognitive processing, suggesting that video games have negative consequences, with a key role identified for desensitisation.

- **Kestanbaum and Weinstein (1985)** found that game-playing helped adolescent males to manage developmental conflicts and discharge aggression safely, suggesting that negativity may be mainly a parental concern.
- **Dunn and Hughes (2001)** found that 'difficult' preschoolers who played video games were more likely to engage in violent fantasy play than children without behavioural difficulties, suggesting that individual differences should be considered.
- **Gee (2003)** found that game-playing correlated positively with development of problem-solving ability, individualism and creativity, emphasising the educational value of game-playing.
- **Eisenberg and Fabes (1998)** reported younger children to be more at risk of harm from violent video games as they were still constructing their moral scaffolding, suggesting that the values operating in violent video games have a greater impact on such children than on older individuals with established value systems.
- **Sopes and Millar (1983)** found that children playing video games exhibited addictive tendencies due to the compulsive behavioural involvement and exhibited withdrawal symptoms, such as the shakes, when attempting to stop playing. They also turned to crime to fund their habit.
- **Sanger (1996)** found that game-playing helped develop a sense of mastery and control in individuals with low self-esteem, suggesting a positive practical application.

Evaluation

- Cooley-Quille et al. (2001) report evidence suggesting that exposure to video-game violence alters cognitive, affective and behavioural processes.
- Cantor (2000) believes that video games demonstrate and reinforce aggressive actions, leading to negative cognitive and behavioural effects.
- Research has not identified those most at risk of negative impact when playing video games and under what conditions negative impacts are more likely.
- Eron (2001) suggests that emotional desensitisation blunts empathetic response, while cognitive desensitisation causes stronger pro-violence attitudes.
- Evidence from video games research suggests cause for concern over children's exposure to them, as empathy development is retarded and moral evaluation is non-existent while pro-violence attitudes and behaviour are constantly reinforced.
- Evidence suggests that the experience of video games contributes to the construction of an individual's reality, with an acceptance of violence merged with desensitisation to its consequences.
- Desensitisation to violence is difficult to measure objectively and researchers instead measure related characteristics that they expect to be affected. Such measures may not therefore be completely valid.
- Relationships have been identified between exposure to violent video games and desensitisation. However, these are only correlational and do not show causality.
- Most studies are of Western cultures, so results may not be generalisable to other cultural groupings.

Examiner tip

There is a common perception that video games and computers have a negative influence on behaviour, which means students often focus too much, or even completely, on negative aspects. Better answers create a more balanced view by focusing additionally on positive effects, for which there is much research support.

- Studies have not really focused on the long-term effects of game-playing.
- Gee (2003) argues that game-playing offers opportunities for experiential learning experiences, especially in developing social and cultural learning and reasoning skills.

Computers

Computer-based media such as the internet, e-mails, blogs, websites and games are a constantly growing source of influence. Interest has focused on relationships that lack face-to-face communication, with other research concentrating on learning effects. Computers can be a positive tool for communicating, learning and developing social relationships in those lacking social skills and confidence and those living in remote communities, though deception can be difficult to detect. There is also the possibility of deindividuation, leading to disinhibition, causing individuals to act in non-typical ways.

computers a medium of communication involving programmable electronic machines

Research

- **Durkin and Barber (2002)** found evidence of positive outcomes in 16-year-olds playing computer games. Measures of family closeness, activity involvement, school engagement, mental health, lack of substance misuse and friendship networks were superior in game-players than non-playing peers, suggesting that computers can be a positive feature of a healthy adolescence.
- **Pearce (2007)** presented the same information to students via either printed paper (group A) or a film of the printed paper (group B) or displayed on a computer screen (group C). Group A recalled 85% of the information, group B 27% and group C 4%, suggesting that computers are a poor medium for such learning.
- **Alexander and Currie (2004)** found that the amount of computer use in young Scots was related to the incidence of upper body discomfort and headaches, implying a health education issue.
- **Valkenburg and Peter (2009)** found that social network sites promote communication skills and relationship building and aid self-disclosure in shy adolescents, illustrating the value of computers in developing sociability and relationship skills.
- **Rao and Lim (2000)** found deception to be common in computer-mediated communication (CMC) because cues to deception (such as posture shifts) are not transmitted, suggesting that deceptions are harder to detect.
- **McGrath and Hollingshead (1995)** found that CMC requires a lower level of cooperation than visual and audio forms, suggesting that e-mailing may hinder cooperative negotiations. **Rangaswamy and Shell (1997)**, however, found no differences in the nature of outcomes communicated in computer and non-computer mediums.
- **Caspi and Gorsky (2006)** found that Israeli participants believed online deception to be common but only one-third reported using deception, with frequent users, younger users and more competent users being the main culprits. Those using deception felt that it created a sense of harmless enjoyment, suggesting that CMC is changing personal moral standards.

- **Keisler and Sproull (1992)** found that CMC led to disinhibition, with users becoming more selfish and self-concerned, and lacking in empathetic feeling for the welfare of others. But they also found that anonymity could help those with social inhibitions to communicate across social and psychological boundaries, suggesting that CMC can have positive and negative effects.
- **Walther (1993)** found that people using CMC exhibited more disinhibition, in the form of non-typical swearing, insults and hostile swearing.

Evaluation

- Fanning (2007) believes our early years are important for constructing knowledge structures, allowing the learning of abstract, metaphoric and symbolic types of information. The constant use of computers can negatively affect this development.
- Behrmann (2000) argues that computers can be beneficial if children are encouraged to engage in social interactions and stimulated to acquire knowledge.
- Differences in research findings concerning the effects of computers on communication and negotiation may be due to differences in the types of CMC used, for example e-mailing and instant messaging. Different systems involve varying amounts of time between receiving and sending messages, creating differences in the levels of reasoning required of responses, and affecting messages sent.
- Van Gelder (1985) reports on the case of 'Joan', a well-regarded member of an online group of disabled people who developed strong platonic and romantic cyber relationships with other members but was ultimately revealed to be an able-bodied man in his 50s seeking to explore the intimacy of female friendships. This highlights the risk of deception for young people engaging in CMC.
- Zhou et al. (2001) found significant cues in CMC indicating the use of deception and believe these could be incorporated into an automated tool which would detect deception and protect young people from those with negative intentions.
- Research into deception within CMC is based on online questionnaires, which could be eliciting idealised and socially desirable answers, suggesting that the findings may not be valid.

> **Knowledge check 2**
>
> In what positive and negative ways can video games and computers affect behaviour?

Persuasion, attitude and change

Specification content

- *The application of Hovland–Yale and Elaboration Likelihood models in explaining the persuasive effects of media*
- *Explanations for the persuasiveness of television advertising*

You should note the necessity to study the Hovland–Yale and Elaboration Likelihood models because both are named and could feature as explicit requirements of a question. Attention then switches to explaining how effective television advertising is, with students expected to be able to outline and evaluate such explanations.

The application of Hovland–Yale and Elaboration Likelihood models in explaining the persuasive effects of media

attitude a predisposition towards an object or situation that prompts individuals to act in a certain way

Hovland–Yale model an explanation of attitude change as a sequence of stages in response to a communication

An **attitude** is a disposition towards an object or situation, prompting individuals to behave in certain ways. Social psychologists became interested in attitude change during the Second World War as the mass media became increasingly influential.

Hovland–Yale model (1953)

The **Hovland–Yale model** focuses on the role of persuasion, perceiving attitude change as a response to communication. Research done at Yale University identified several important factors.

- **Target characteristics** relate to the individual receiving and processing communications, with less intelligent individuals seen as being more easily persuadable. Self-esteem is another important characteristic, with individuals of moderate levels being more easily persuaded than those of high or low levels. Mood also features as a key characteristic.
- **Source characteristics** focus on the credibility of the communicator, with more credible communicators seen as more persuasive, though there is some argument as to whether this is a short- or long-term effect. Credibility focuses on the expertise, trustworthiness and attractiveness of the communicator.
- **Message characteristics** concentrate on the nature of the communication, with presentation of both sides of an argument being seen as a more persuasive method of creating attitude change.

Overall, attitude change is perceived as a sequential process comprising stages of **attention** (the target attends to the message), **comprehension** (the target understands the message), **reactance** (the target reacts to the message either positively or negatively) and **acceptance** (the message is accepted if perceived as credible).

Research

- **Rhodes and Woods (1992)** found people with moderate self-esteem levels to be more persuadable than those with high and low levels, suggesting an inverted-U relationship between self-esteem and persuadability. **Janis (1954)** found contradictory evidence, that those of low self-esteem were more persuadable.
- **Hovland and Weiss (1951)** found evidence of a 'sleeper effect', where attitude change due to credible source characteristics was short-lasting.

- **Allyn and Festinger (1961)** found that distracting people made them more persuadable than when their full attention was captured, suggesting a strategy to achieve attitude change.
- **Walster and Festinger (1962)** found that deliberately targeted messages were less persuasive.
- **Meveritz and Chaiken (1987)** discovered that messages designed to scare people were more effective in persuading changes in attitude, suggesting that fear plays a role in effective attitude change. However, people would ignore very frightening messages.

Evaluation

- The 'sleeper effect' (where attitude changes occurring due to a credible communicator are short term) is demonstrated when an individual is told a message and then its source, and not vice versa.
- The model describes the process of attitude change rather than explaining it.
- Research concerning the model tends to be laboratory based, showing causality and allowing for replication. However, due to the artificial environment findings may not be truly valid.
- Research exploring the role of fear in persuasive messages can be seen as harmful and therefore unethical.

Elaboration Likelihood model: Petty and Cacioppo (1986)

The Elaboration Likelihood model explains how persuasive messages are processed and perceives two different forms of **cognitive routes** by which persuasive attitude change can occur through cognitive evaluation.

(1) **Central route** — this occurs when an individual is presented with material and is motivated to analyse it carefully to reach an attitude-changing conclusion. This route is used for important messages requiring elaborated cognitive effort. Such messages need to be robust, as persuasion is influenced by the quality of the message. If favourable thoughts are produced, attitude change is likely.

(2) **Peripheral route** — this occurs when an individual is motivated to consider the source of a communication to change an attitude rather than the message itself. This route only considers superficial cues, such as the perceived credibility of the communicator and the quality of the presentation, with the logic behind the message seen as irrelevant and with no elaboration required.

As motivation and the ability to process a message increase, it becomes more likely that the central route will be used, though with moderate elaboration a mixture of central and peripheral routes are used. Motivational factors include personal relevance of the message, accountability and an individual's innate desire to indulge in thinking. Ability factors include the availability of cognitive resources (such as distractions) and the relevant knowledge necessary to analyse arguments.

Knowledge check 3
Summarise the Hovland–Yale model in explaining the persuasiveness of media.

Examiner tip
The focus of the specification is not merely on describing and evaluating the Hovland–Yale and Elaboration Likelihood models, but instead concentrates on the application of the models in explaining the persuasive effects of media. Therefore, studying and revising should be concentrated on this explicit requirement, as that is what questions will be asked about.

Elaboration Likelihood model an explanation of how persuasive messages are processed through cognitive evaluation

Knowledge check 4
Summarise the Elaboration Likelihood model in explaining the persuasiveness of media.

Research

- **Miller (2005)** found that peripheral route processing relied on environmental conditions, such as perceived credibility of the source, quality of its presentation, attractiveness of the source and catchy slogans, supporting the model.
- **Petty et al. (1976)** found that low distraction leads to more agreement than high distraction with a strong communication, but to less agreement with weak communication, suggesting that the ability to process messages determines whether central or peripheral routes are used.
- **Chaiken (1980)** found that participants were more likely to retain new attitudes achieved via persuasion if the attitude change was acquired by the central route, suggesting that attitude change is greater when the central route is used.
- **Petty et al. (1981)** found that students were most influenced by persuasive messages when they were personally motivated and by peripheral cues when not personally motivated.

Examiner tip

Many students will study and revise the Hovland–Yale and Elaboration Likelihood models separately. However, an effective way of creating high-level evaluative material is to compare them, drawing out similarities/differences and strengths/weaknesses. There might even be an exam question specifically requiring such comparison, so be prepared for this.

Evaluation

- Although the model has explanatory power, it lacks predictive ability in different contexts.
- The model has addressed its criticisms by being continually updated.
- Chaiken (1980) proposes a **heuristic-systematic model** using two processing modes. Communications can either be attended to carefully by analytical systematic processing, or by the use of heuristic mental shortcuts, such as using stereotypes to make decisions. This alternative model permits a wider range of specific predictions.

Explanations for the effectiveness of television advertising

The Hovland–Yale and Elaboration Likelihood models of attitude change can both be used as explanations for the effectiveness of television advertising.

Hovland–Yale model

There are three factors that can be used to explain the effectiveness of television advertising.

(1) **Communicator** — television advertising often uses skilled communicators possessing attractive qualities. Constant exposure to such figures increases their persuasiveness as we identify with and look up to them, as well as coming to see them as trustworthy.

(2) **Message** — the means by which a message is communicated is a strong factor, with television advertising being especially influential due to its immediacy and ever-increasing availability (e.g. increased number of channels). The persuasiveness of television advertising works best for simple messages, with alternative means such as written media being better for complex messages as they allow recipients to revisit the material.

(3) Audience — there appears to be a gender difference in the persuadability of television audiences, with males being more persuadable by female-based topics and females being more persuadable by male-based topics. Research has also indicated that age-related differences may exist.

Research

- **Hugo-Saylor et al. (1992)** found that preschoolers' themes of play were 'hurricane based' following television coverage of a hurricane, suggesting that receiver-response characteristics may be age dependent.
- **Chaiken and Eagly (1983)** found that presentation of easily comprehensible messages created the greatest attitude change when viewed on video, while complex messages led to bigger attitude changes when viewed in a written format, suggesting that the persuasiveness of television advertising is dependent on the complexity of a message.
- **Sistrunk and McDavid (1971)** found that female-orientated television topics had more of a persuasive effect on male attitudes than female attitudes, suggesting a gender difference in the persuasiveness of television advertising.
- **Eagly and Carli (1981)** found that women were more influenced by messages that contained unfamiliar content, suggesting a gender difference in receptiveness to television advertising.

Evaluation

- Petty and Cacioppo (1981) found that communicators who are trustworthy, attractive, credible and similar to the recipient create greater attitude change. These findings have been successfully used from a practical point of view in television anti-smoking campaigns.
- The ability of communicators who have positive qualities and similarities to the audience to produce attitude change can also be explained in terms of social learning theory, where the audience observes and imitates the communicator as a form of vicarious reinforcement.
- Whether a message is one- or two-sided also has an effect on attitude change. Hovland et al. (1949) found that one-sided messages produced greater attitude change in those of low educational achievement, while two-sided messages produced greater change in those of higher educational achievement. This suggests that advertisers should consider the intellect of their target audience.

Elaboration Likelihood model

More effective persuasion comes from using the central route where an individual is motivated to analyse material carefully. Messages therefore have to be robust and personally important so that they require elaborated cognitive effort. The use of strong arguments when presenting material, encouraging people to analyse and think about points being made, as well as cutting out any possible distractions, can help to achieve this.

The peripheral route, where the source of the communication rather than the message itself is considered, also plays a role in the effectiveness of television persuasiveness,

Examiner tip
Some students find it difficult to evaluate explanations for the persuasiveness of television advertising and resort to compiling a list of unconnected, unexplained points. Better answers will compare explanations, drawing out differences and similarities as a form of elaborated commentary that shows real insight. This will earn high-level credit.

with people in contented moods more likely to use this route as they wish to maintain their positive emotive state.

Audiences must first have their attention captured and this can be done by the use of heightened emotions such as fear, though too much fear can put people on the defensive and thus make them unwilling to elaborate their cognitive processing.

Research

- **Witte and Allen (2000)** found that messages with a strong fear and high efficacy content produced the greatest change in attitudes in anti-smoking campaigns.
- **Leventhal et al. (1967)** found that, if a pamphlet on how to stop smoking was used after a fear reaction had been provoked by a hard-hitting anti-smoking film, then attitude change was possible as the pamphlet reduced the fear response, allowing elaborated cognitive processing to occur.
- **Petty and Cacioppo (1986)** investigated the multiple roles notion, where any given variable influences attitudes by different processes at different points along the elaboration continuum. Thus, with high elaboration, the use of beautiful scenery in an advertisement for a holiday is influential due to its relevance but has decreased impact when used in a car advertisement due to its irrelevance. However, with low elaboration beautiful scenery has an equally positive effect in both scenarios.
- **Gorn and Goldberg (1980)** found that moderate message repetition was effective as it presented more opportunity for elaborated scrutiny. However, over-usage was ineffective, as it produced tedium.

Evaluation

- Griskevicius et al. (2009) asked participants to watch either a romantic or a frightening film, followed by an advertisement using either conformity or uniqueness as a persuasive tool. Those watching the romantic film were more persuaded by uniqueness, while those watching the frightening film were more persuaded by conformity, suggesting that advertisements could be tailored to fit the programmes they follow.
- There is a body of opinion that considers the use of psychological models and methods to achieve attitude change through television advertising to be unethical as people are being manipulated without their informed consent (i.e. by propaganda rather than education).
- The use of psychological models and methods as persuasive elements is especially important in programmes that involve debates and viewer participation, such as public health campaigns.

Knowledge check 5

How can the Hovland–Yale and Elaboration Likelihood models explain the persuasiveness of television advertising?

The psychology of celebrity

Specification content

- *The attraction of 'celebrity', including social psychological and evolutionary explanations*
- *Research into intense fandom, including celebrity worship and celebrity stalking*

There is a requirement to study both social psychological and evolutionary explanations of celebrity, as both are explicitly named and may feature directly in examination questions, as is the case with celebrity worship and celebrity stalking, which again are specifically listed and may therefore also feature directly in questions, though any other relevant material would be of equal merit.

Celebrities are widely recognised individuals with a high public profile, including those famous just for being famous. The obsession with celebrity can be found in all forms of media and has aroused considerable debate about its influence upon society in general and upon specific groups such as children, with modern phenomena such as stalking arousing concern. Various psychological theories have been offered as explanations, including social psychological and evolutionary ones.

Social psychological explanations for the attraction of celebrity

- **Social learning theory (SLT)** — we continually observe celebrities in the media and as they often have qualities causing us to identify with them as role models, we may imitate them due to vicarious reinforcement.
- **Social identity theory (SIT)** — collective admiration of celebrities and membership of fan clubs and internet discussion groups can create in-group and out-group membership as part of an individual's social identity.
- **Social construction theory** — social phenomena are seen as constructions by those within a culture or society, which are then maintained through social interactions. Therefore, celebrity is perceived as a self-serving, social invention of the media, providing continual interest and focus (maintenance) that generates substantial income.
- **Absorption–addiction model** — individuals develop interest in celebrities due to a lack of meaningful relationships within their lives and as an attempt to escape mundane reality. Thus interest in celebrities can be perceived as an attempt to gain a more positive self-identity and feel fulfilled. In stronger forms the interest in celebrity can become addictive, with individuals feeling a need for more involvement with celebrities and such a need correlating strongly with diminished psychological health.
- **Positive–active model** — interest in celebrities is seen in a positive light, as it entails involvement in active participation, such as creating and participating in social networks (e.g. fan clubs and forums), which can enhance social skills.

celebrities people familiar to the public

social psychological explanations explanations of attraction that are based upon the social influence of celebrity

> ### Research
>
> - **Chamberlain et al. (2009)** examined the idea that, due to social power and status, celebrities received more favourable treatment in law courts. However, no differences were found between the treatment of celebrities and non-celebrities, suggesting that the social impact of celebrities may be less than imagined.
> - **Escalis and Bettman (2008)** found that celebrity endorsement enhanced a product when consumers aspired to be like the celebrity, suggesting support for social psychological explanations, especially that of SLT. A second study found consumers self-enhanced by building connections to favourable celebrities and distancing themselves from unfavourable celebrity images, again supporting social psychological explanations.

- **Derrick and Gabriel (2008)** found that parasocial relationships were beneficial to those who had difficulties with interpersonal relationships. Admiring celebrities enhanced self-esteem, bringing individuals closer to the ideals they held about themselves.
- **Belch and Belch (2007)** found that celebrities were often well liked, leading to identification in an attempt to seek a kind of relationship with the celebrity, supporting the absorption–addiction model.
- **Richins (1994)** found that individuals identified with celebrities to help construct their self-concepts and identities, supporting social psychological explanations.
- **Kaminer (2005)** reported that 'love' for a pop star or athlete may compensate for the absence of genuine romantic attachments or other actual, intimate relationships, supporting the absorption–addiction model.

Evaluation

- The fact that 20% of advertisements in the USA feature celebrities suggests a social learning effect.
- Crocker and Park (2004) believe that people have an interest in celebrities as they are motivated to have a favourable self-identity and a need to maintain and enhance self-esteem.
- Kaminer (2005) believes relationships between fans can create relationships of intimacy like those between friends or family, supporting the positive–active model. She also perceives a victory for a favoured sports team as bringing together different people towards a common goal (the victory) and a common foe (the opposing team) suggesting support for SIT.
- The majority of research into the attraction of celebrity has been done in Western cultures and so findings may be culturally specific.
- De Backer et al. (2007) believe that celebrities are viewed as higher-status members of society and are therefore used for behaviour modelling. Mass media audiences gossip about celebrities to learn about them and thus emulate them, with the motivation that imitation will raise an individual's status.

Knowledge check 6

How can the attraction of celebrity be explained through social psychological means?

Evolutionary explanations for the attraction of celebrity

Evolutionary explanations perceiving the attractiveness of celebrity as serving an adaptive function

Evolutionary explanations see celebrity as serving an adaptive function and therefore bestowing a survival value. The majority of human evolution occurred in the Pleistocene era, also known as the environment of evolutionary adaptiveness (EEA). Therefore, behaviours linked to the attractiveness of celebrities may be adaptive to that past environment rather than the present. Evolutionary theory sees any behaviour aiding survival and reproduction as being acted upon by natural selection to become more widespread throughout the population. Evolution also explains the fact that people become celebrities because of their attractive qualities, such qualities giving them an adaptive advantage in gaining better access to resources.

- **Gossip** — language evolved to fulfil several functions, one of which was the communication of social information within a group. Dunbar (1997) believes that in the EEA groups grew so large that gossip became the most effective manner of communicating information about social relationships and hierarchies. This explains the unending appeal of celebrity journalism in communicating observations about alpha males and females. Just as we are hard-wired by evolution to consume as much food as possible, so evolution also attracts us to 'consume' as much celebrity gossip as possible.
- **Attractiveness** — evolutionary theory sees attractiveness as being adaptive, entailing better reproduction opportunities and therefore offering survival value. Interest in celebrities focuses on their enhanced attractiveness, the reason for their lofty status.
- **Gender** — interest in celebrity tends to be a more female-orientated social feature and evolution explains this as allowing females to compare and focus upon desirable males as a means of selection. Female interest in female celebrities can be seen as females competing in levels of attractiveness, as well as learning attractiveness skills from alpha females.
- **Prestige hypothesis** — individuals benefit from imitating prestigious (high-status) people. Such imitation may bring an individual more resources, protection and reproductive opportunities, therefore having an adaptive value.

Research

- **Dunbar (1997)** reported that two-thirds of conversation was spent on social topics, supporting the idea that language evolved for social purposes.
- **Fieldman (2008)** reported that females found male celebrities attractive because of qualities advertising toughness, stamina and high levels of testosterone, all indicators of good genetic quality and an ability to provide resources.
- **Fox (2009)** reported that gossiping about celebrities involved treating them as members of the participants' own social group.
- **Morin et al. (2008)** found that females were more influenced by celebrities endorsing products, supporting the idea of interest in celebrity being a more female- than male-orientated feature.
- **De Backer et al. (2005)** found that interest in celebrity gossip was a by-product of an evolved mechanism useful for acquiring survival information relevant to fitness.

Evaluation

- Celebrity journalism often focuses on attractiveness, romantic liaisons and reproductive success, supporting the idea that attraction to celebrity has an evolutionary basis.
- Dunbar (1997) sees celebrity attraction as related to a need to prevent social free-loading, where individuals receive more resources than they provide.
- Reynolds (2009) believes evolution programmes us to find certain individuals attractive because we share similar genes and thus have the same perception of beauty, suggesting a reason why celebrities are universally popular.

Knowledge check 7

How can the attraction of celebrity be explained through evolutionary means?

Examiner tip

Care should be taken when answering questions on evolutionary explanations that the focus is not just on explaining the theory of evolution, but instead on how evolutionary theory can explain the attraction of celebrity. This applies equally to evaluative as well as to descriptive material, for example, focusing on the degree of research support for evolutionary explanations.

- **Maltby et al. (2005)** found an interaction between intense-personal celebrity worship and body image in female adolescents aged between 14 and 16, suggesting that parasocial relationships with celebrities seen as having positive body images leads to negative body images in female adolescents and possible eating disorders. However, this effect appeared to be short lived, generally disappearing with the onset of adulthood.
- **McCutcheon (2006)** found no relationship between childhood attachment patterns and mild forms of celebrity worship, suggesting that such interests are not formed by childhood tendencies.
- **McCutcheon and Houran (2003)** found that one third of people suffered from **celebrity worship syndrome**, a fascination with the lives of the rich and the famous. From a sample of more than 600 participants, 20% followed celebrities in the media for entertainment-social reasons, with such people tending to have extrovert personalities. A further 10% developed an intense-personal attitude towards celebrities, tending to be neurotic, tense, emotional and moody while 1% of participants were classed as borderline-pathological. This group exhibited impulsive, antisocial, egocentric behaviour indicative of psychosis, suggesting that while celebrity worship does not make someone dysfunctional it increases their chances of being so. The researchers believe that people develop interests in celebrities when they are looking for direction in their lives (as in adolescence) or as a response to the loss of someone close.

> **Knowledge check 8**
> Explain how intense fandom can have both healthy and unhealthy effects.

Evaluation

- Much research into celebrity worship uses questionnaires. Although these allow lots of information to be collected relatively quickly, they tend to be affected by socially desirable and idealised answers and can therefore lack validity.
- Mild forms of celebrity worship can be potentially beneficial. Larsen (1995) found that intense attachments to celebrities provide young people with attitudinal and behavioural exemplars.
- Maltby's (2002) entertainment-social dimension of fandom is consistent with Stever's (1991) observation that fans are attracted to celebrities due to their perceived ability to entertain and capture attention.
- West and Sweeting (2002) recommend media training in schools to illustrate the dangers of celebrity worship and eating disorders, especially in adolescent girls.
- MacDougal (2005) suggests that the veneration given to dead celebrities by some fans is like that found in charismatic religions.

Celebrity stalking

Research

- **McCutcheon et al. (2006)** used various measurements of attachment patterns and attraction to celebrities and, while finding no relationship between these and mild celebrity worship, did find that adults with insecure attachment types tended to have positive attitudes towards obsessive behaviours and celebrity stalking. A worrying correlation between pathological attachment types and a tendency to stalk was also found, suggesting that stalking behaviour is linked to childhood attachment patterns.

> **celebrity stalking**
> following or watching a celebrity persistently due to an obsession

- **Morris (2002)** found stalking to be an activity mainly conducted by males, with most victims being not celebrities but ex-intimate partners, though some offenders indulged in serial stalking. Ten per cent of women and 4% of men have been victims of stalking, rising to 17% of women and 7% of men if the definition is widened to 'persistent and unwanted attention'. Most victims suffer deterioration in their health and serious psychological impacts and have to make significant changes to their lives, like moving house or changing jobs, suggesting that stalking is a fairly common problem with serious consequences and is not a phenomenon limited to celebrities.
- **Kamphuis and Emmelkamp (2000)** found that 25% of stalking cases culminated in violence, with 2% leading to murder. However, there were variations between types of stalkers:
  - the erotomanic stalker, usually female (with a delusional belief that an older man of status or celebrity is in love with her)
  - the obsessional stalker (who stalks after a real relationship has gone sour)
  - the resentful stalker (who stalks to frighten and distress)
  - the predatory stalker (who may precipitate sexual attacks)
  - the psychotic stalker (who targets famous people)

  This suggests that the general label of 'stalker' is too wide, there appearing to be several types of stalker with different profiles who indulge in stalking for different reasons and that only some types of stalking involve celebrities.
- **McCutcheon et al. (2006)** developed the **obsessive relational intrusion and celebrity stalking scale** as a measurement of celebrity stalking. Using factor analysis, the scale was found to have two subscales labelled 'persistent pursuit' and 'threat'. The scale has proven reliability and validity and because it uses indirect measurements is perceived as being free from social desirability bias.
- **Mullen (2008)** scrutinised 20,000 incidents of stalking the royal family, finding that 80% of instances involved people with serious psychotic disorders (e.g. schizophrenia). The characteristics of those who stalk non-famous people are very different, suggesting that celebrity stalking is a separate phenomenon from other forms of the behaviour.

Examiner tip
When answering questions on research studies into intense fandom, many students simply describe studies in terms of aims/procedures/findings. This gains marks for description but not for evaluation. To gain evaluative credit, you must comment on the methodology or state what the findings tell us about intense fandom (e.g. they suggest that celebrity stalking is related to childhood attachment patterns).

Evaluation

- Care should be taken to address the ethical concern of potential harm when researching into people with possible pathological tendencies. A thorough debriefing should be administered with provision also made for appropriate support if needed.
- Research into celebrity stalking may create an understanding of the behaviour, leading to the formation of effective treatments and therapies.
- Suggested treatments for celebrity stalkers include psychotherapy to address the root causes, with a role also for drug treatments to reduce obsessive tendencies.
- Giles (2002) believes that there is an implicit tendency to see individuals who indulge in behaviours like celebrity stalking as pathological. However, although relationships with media celebrities are imaginary, they do lead to attitudinal and behavioural changes.
- Research into stalking is problematic, as definitions vary from country to country, making even simple estimates of its frequency difficult.

- Obsessive, rejected stalkers have responded favourably to psychotherapy, but psychopathic stalkers who prey on celebrities have proven highly resistant to treatment, indicating that different forms of stalking may be separate from each other.
- Legal intervention, such as a trespassing order, appears to be the best way of dealing with celebrity stalkers, but this can often stimulate such stalkers into even more malicious and persecutory behaviour.

Knowledge check 9

What are the characteristics of celebrity stalkers?

- Media influence both pro- and antisocial behaviour through social learning theory, cognitive priming, stereotyping, desensitisation and displacement, while computers and video games also incur both positive and negative effects.
- The Hovland–Yale model of persuasion perceives attitude change as a response to communication, while the Elaboration Likelihood model sees persuasive messages as processed through central and peripheral routes, with attitude change occurring through cognitive evaluation.
- Both the Hovland–Yale and Elaboration Likelihood models can be used to explain the persuasiveness of television advertising.

- Social psychological explanations for the attraction of celebrity include social learning theory, social identity theory, social construction theory, the absorption-addiction model, as well as the positive-active model, while evolutionary explanations see adaptive advantages to being attracted to celebrity that increase chances of survival.
- Research has identified different categories of celebrity worship and dimensions of fandom and suggested motivations behind celebrity stalking, which differs from other forms of stalking.

Summary

The psychology of addictive behaviour

Models of addictive behaviour

Specification content

- *Biological, cognitive and learning approaches to explaining initiation, maintenance and relapse, and their applications to smoking and gambling*

The specification focuses on several theoretical explanations of initiation, maintenance and relapse and, as these are explicitly listed, they could form a direct requirement of examination questions. The focus then moves on to applications of these approaches to two specific addictions, smoking and gambling, which again could form the basis of examination questions.

Biological model of addiction

Addiction occurs when a person becomes reliant upon something to function normally. The biological model perceives such addiction as a physiologically

addiction a dependency on something physically or psychologically habit-forming

biological model addiction is seen as occurring as a physiologically controlled pattern of behaviour

controlled pattern of behaviour. The initiation of addiction is seen as occurring by genetic vulnerability triggered by environmental stressors, while maintenance of addiction occurs through the activation of dopamine, upon which some drugs, like cocaine, have a direct effect. Relapse is explained as due to physiological cravings.

Drugs affect the nervous system, especially synapses, in several ways by reducing or increasing the frequency of nerve impulses. They can block neurotransmitter receptor sites or attach to receptors so that they have the same effect as a neurotransmitter, or they can prevent neurotransmitters from recycling so that they remain in the synapse and re-attach to receptor sites.

Research

- **Overstreet et al. (1993)** found that different genetic strains of rats demonstrated differences in levels of liking for alcohol, suggesting that preference for alcohol is under genetic control.
- **Nielsen et al. (2008)** compared DNA from former heroin addicts and non-addicts and found a relationship between addiction and certain gene variants. Some genes also seemed to act against the process of addiction. These differences in behaviour patterns indicate a genetic basis to addiction.
- **Kendler and Prescott (1998)** interviewed 1,934 female twins between the ages of 22 and 62 and found that, although family and environmental factors were influential, progression from casual use of marijuana and cocaine to addiction was due mainly to genetic factors, suggesting that dependence is highly heritable.
- **Van den Bree et al. (1998)** studied 188 twin pairs, finding that dependency was greatly influenced by genetic factors, but especially so for males. In females genetic influences accounted for 47% of differences between identical and fraternal twins, rising to 79% in males, suggesting that there is a gender difference in dependency vulnerability.

Knowledge check 10

How does the biological model explain addiction, especially to smoking and gambling?

Evaluation

- The model relies heavily on evidence from animal studies, which may not be generalisable to humans.
- Biological explanations are incomplete, as they do not consider the important role that psychological factors play.
- There is a wealth of evidence from research into genetics, twin and family studies supporting the biological model, indicating the existence of biological predispositions towards addiction.
- The model is better able to explain physical addictions (such as drugs) than other types, although addictions such as gambling can also be explained by biological means.
- Addiction to one drug can produce cross-tolerance of other related drugs (opiates). The withdrawal symptoms associated with abstaining from an addicted drug can be addressed by taking a similar drug (e.g. methadone in the place of heroin). This suggests that similar drugs act upon the nervous system in the same way, supporting the biological model.

Examiner tip

Rather than studying and revising models of addiction separately, a good means of creating high-level evaluative material is to compare the theories, drawing out similarities/differences and strengths/weaknesses. There might even be an exam question specifically requiring such comparison, so be prepared for this.

Cognitive model of addiction

The cognitive model sees addiction as due to distorted thinking relating to dysfunctional beliefs about drug use, for example that intellectual functioning is dependent on drug use. These maladaptive cognitive processes may relate to mood, causing addicts to believe that happiness is impossible without the drug. Dysfunctional beliefs can be self-fulfilling, leading to a perception of personal incapability in controlling drug usage, in turn leading to an inability to direct attention away from addictive behaviour.

Faulty thinking also leads the addict to focus on positive features of drug use and to minimise negative ones, again strengthening dependency. Another cognitive feature is impaired decision-making ability. Addicts classically focus on strategies of immediate pleasure, even with the knowledge that such choices will be harmful in the long term.

The model therefore sees initiation, maintenance and relapse as due to maladaptive thought processes.

cognitive model
addiction is seen as occurring through distorted thinking related to dysfunctional beliefs

Research

- **Grant et al. (1996)**, using brain scans, found increased activity in areas of the frontal cortex associated with decision making during periods of craving, suggesting that the cognitive and biological models can be linked.
- **McCusker (2001)** found that an individual's concept of the importance of things was related to addiction increase, leading addicts to perceive things related to their dependency selectively, thus activating expectations concerning the positive effects of their addictive behaviour. This expectation led to a perception of craving, suggesting that the model can explain how addictions are maintained and why relapses occur.
- **Hester and Garavan (2005)** reported that, as thoughts of drug use are in working memory, attention also remained focused on relevant environmental features, which in turn maintained thoughts relating to drug use within working memory. This suggests that addictive behaviours and cravings become self-perpetuating.
- **Koski-Jannes (1992)** found that addictions can form from short-sighted means of dealing with stressful situations, giving initially positive but later negative consequences, leading to a self-perpetuating cycle of addiction regulated by self-serving thoughts. This suggests that the cognitive model can explain how addictions are initiated.
- **Ratelle et al. (2004)** used a questionnaire to find that gambling addicts had persistent thoughts about gambling and poorer concentration on daily tasks, indicating a cognitive element to addiction.

Knowledge check 11

How does the cognitive model explain addiction, especially to smoking and gambling?

Evaluation

- The biological model is a better explanation of the initiation of dependency, but the cognitive model more ably accounts for maintenance and relapses.
- Cognitive models offer incomplete explanations, being based upon expectations and beliefs, thus ignoring important biological factors.

- The relative success of cognitive-behavioural treatments suggests that addiction must have a cognitive component.
- Ryle (1990) believes that 'dilemmas' in which alternatives are seen in too limited a manner (e.g. 'without drugs I'd have no friends') and 'snags', where we abandon appropriate aims due to perceiving them as dissatisfactory (e.g. 'I would abstain but...') create mental obstacles to changing addictive behaviour. This suggests that any successful treatment must address such dilemmas and snags.

Learning models of addiction

learning models addiction is seen as occurring through environmental interactions that produce euphoric outcomes

Learning models see addictive behaviour as being explained by classical conditioning, operant conditioning and social learning theory. With classical conditioning, drug abuse becomes associated with certain environmental factors until those factors alone produce a 'high'. Operant conditioning sees addiction arising from positive reinforcements, such as euphoric drug 'highs', and negative reinforcements, like a reduction in anxiety, serving to strengthen the addictive behaviour by increasing the chances of it recurring. Increased drug usage can be perceived as an attempt to increase these reinforcements. The neurotransmitter dopamine has especially been identified as a reinforcer within the **brain reward system**, with many drugs acting upon dopamine synapses to produce the sensation of euphoria.

SLT sees addiction resulting from vicarious learning, where dependent behaviour is observed and imitated if seen to bring about some form of reinforcing reward in the model.

Learning models therefore see initiation, maintenance and relapse as due to learning experiences involving environmental interactions.

Examiner tip

When outlining and evaluating the learning model, it is important to focus on explaining the initiation, maintenance and relapse of addiction, rather than just outlining and evaluating elements of the model such as classical and operant conditioning and social learning theory.

Research

- **White and Hiroi (1993)** found that rats preferred locations where they had previously received injections of amphetamines, suggesting that 'place preference' is learned by a process of association.
- **Meyer et al. (1995)** found that the sight of a hypodermic needle created positive feelings in addicts, demonstrating the role of classical conditioning in addictive behaviour.
- **Olds (1958)** found that rats with an electrode introduced into certain brain areas, especially the nucleus accumbens, press a lever in a Skinner box up to 2,000 times a minute until collapsing, suggesting a link between biological and learning factors.
- **Farber et al. (1980)** found an important difference between alcohol use through negative reinforcement (escape drinking) and positive reinforcement (social drinking), suggesting that particular learning factors may be more linked to addiction.
- **Bahr et al. (2005)** found from research on over 4,000 American teenagers that drug taking by peers was a big influence in initiating drug use, suggesting an important role for SLT.

Evaluation

- The fact that many abstaining addicts do not experience withdrawal symptoms and cravings suggests that biological factors are not as important as learning ones.
- When researching into addictive behaviour care must be taken to address important and sensitive ethical concerns, for instance it may be the case that addicts cannot really give informed consent. There is also the potential for harm being greatly enhanced.
- Redish (2004) produces a computational learning model of addiction based on the idea that drug taking increases dopamine production as part of a learning–reward system. This model allows predictions to be made and tested, building a better understanding of addiction that may lead to the development of effective treatments.
- Many forms of addiction respond favourably to behavioural treatments, indicating a learning component. However, such treatments often only produce short-term benefits, suggesting that symptoms are being addressed but not causes, implying that other factors must be involved.

Explanations for specific addictions

Smoking

Smoking produces a physical addiction to nicotine, influencing dopamine production and the brain reward system. Statistics from 2006 indicate that over 1 in 5 British people over the age of 16 smoke, with wide differences in how much and how often and how hard people find it to quit. Several explanations have been developed.

- **Biological explanation** — nicotine in cigarettes is seen as affecting the production of the neurotransmitters dopamine and acetylcholine, producing a reinforcing effect. Genetic variations have also been found indicating that some people are more vulnerable than others to dependency.
- **Learning explanations:**
  - **(1) Operant conditioning** — maintenance of smoking can be explained as due to the positive reinforcement produced by the pleasant effect of nicotine inhalation. As nicotine is rapidly removed from the body, frequent reinforcements via smoking are required.
  - **(2) Social learning theory** — initiation of smoking is often seen as occurring via observation and imitation of role models, especially among adolescents, an age when many people first experience smoking. Such people are therefore seen as smoking due to vicarious reinforcement.
- **Cognitive explanation** — smokers are seen as possessing irrational thoughts, for instance that smoking improves cognitive functioning or calms nerves. Such dysfunctional ideas can be self-fulfilling (e.g. not smoking produces anxiety), creating the belief that they cannot quit, leading to a 'vicious circle' of continually giving in to cravings.

Knowledge check 12

How does the learning model explain addiction, especially to smoking and gambling?

Research

- **deCODE Genetics (2006)** found two genetic variations on chromosome 15 that raise the risk of lung cancer in some people and make them strongly addicted to tobacco. This supports the biological model and offers an explanation of why some find it harder to quit.
- **Shiffman (2009)** reported that two-thirds of smokers only indulged occasionally and in certain situations, and had little desire to quit. Most research has concentrated on heavy smokers and may have led to invalid conclusions about smoking addiction. Occasional smokers are not true addicts and thus challenge the idea that smoking is universally addictive.
- **National Institute on Drug Abuse (NIDA) (2005)** found that 90% of American smokers started as adolescents, mainly as a result of observation and imitation of peers, suggesting that initiation of smoking is due to SLT.
- **DiFranza (2007)** found that teenage smokers had strong cravings for smoking only two days after first inhaling, suggesting nicotine to be powerfully dependence forming with long-term use not necessary for addiction.
- **Brynner (1969)** found that media images of smoking created perceptions of it as being attractive and tough, lending support to SLT.
- **Goldberg et al. (1981)** found that monkeys would press a lever in a Skinner box to receive nicotine at a similar rate to that for cocaine, suggesting that smoking is maintained through its reinforcing effect, lending support to operant conditioning as an explanation.
- **NIDA (2005)** reported that acetaldehyde, a chemical in cigarette smoke, contributed to addiction and had age-related effects, with vulnerability to its reinforcing effect being greatest in adolescence. This suggests biological reasons rather than SLT to be responsible for smoking initiation.
- **Pergadia et al. (2006)** found a heritability factor in the experience of nicotine withdrawal symptoms, suggesting a genetic link between smoking experience and thus supporting a biological explanation.
- **Calvert (2009)** reported that smokers shown cigarette packets experienced strong activation in the ventral striatum and nucleus accumbens brain areas, suggesting a biological explanation of craving behaviour.

Evaluation

- A better understanding of smoking addiction has led to the development of medications and treatments to help people quit.
- The fact that biological therapies help people to quit supports the biological explanation.
- Many people quit without using nicotine replacements or suffering cravings, suggesting a role in the addiction for social and cognitive factors.
- Addiction seems to be mainly psychological, there appearing to be little change in nicotine receptors that would characterise biological tolerance.
- Salient cues that draw attention to smoking, like ash trays or the sight of others smoking, can also explain its continuation.

- Reynolds et al. (2008) found a link between smoking and delay discounting (where a person has a preference for a smaller, immediate reward, e.g. a cigarette, than a larger, delayed reward). Whether degree of delay discounting is due to genetic factors or environmental factors is not determined, however.

Gambling

Although gambling addiction does not involve dependency on a physical substance, its symptoms and effects can make it just as much of a dependency behaviour as drug addiction. As with smoking, not all gamblers are classed as addicts and again several explanations for the behaviour have been offered.

- **Cognitive explanation** — irrational thought patterns are seen as distorting beliefs about levels of skill and luck (success can be perceived as due to skill and loss as due to luck or not paying attention). Superstitious beliefs are often developed to account for winning and losing, which can lead to greater risk taking and increased persistence.
- **Biological explanation** — as with physical addictions, gambling increases dopamine production, creating a pleasurable sensation in the brain reward system. Research has also indicated genetic factors to be involved, with some people at risk of developing multiple addictions. Genetics may explain why some gamblers are more at risk of addiction, as genetic inheritance may bestow different levels of dependency vulnerability on people. The idea that personality factors increase the risk of gambling dependency is also explained by genetics.
- **Learning explanation** — gambling behaviour can become associated with particular environmental factors through classical conditioning such as betting when seeing a betting shop, or through operant conditioning by the reinforcement of wins and social learning theory by observation and imitation of those modelling gambling behaviour and seen to be reinforced for doing so.

Research

- **Griffiths (1994)** found that habitual users of fruit machines tended to hold irrational beliefs about losing (like not concentrating) and attributed successes to personal skill, suggesting a cognitive explanation.
- **Roy et al. (2004)** found higher levels of norepinephrine levels in chronic blackjack gamblers and higher levels of dopamine in chronic casino gamblers, showing pronounced activation of the HPA axis and sympathoadrenergic system, suggesting that biological neuroendocrine disturbances can account for dependency.
- **Anholt et al. (2003)** found that problem gamblers had obsessive–compulsive thought patterns, suggesting that dependency can be explained by cognitive factors.
- **Grosset et al. (2009)** found that dopamine agonists used to treat Parkinson's disease were turning 10% of patients into pathological gamblers, suggesting that dopamine is linked to gambling dependency, thus supporting the biological explanation.
- **Eisen et al. (2001)**, using twin studies, found a correlation between heredity and both problem gambling and alcoholism, suggesting that genetic factors may be at play in addictive behaviours generally.

Examiner tip

Read questions on the application of models to explain smoking and gambling carefully, as questions could focus specifically on initiation, maintenance or relapse of one of or both these behaviours, or indeed combinations of these elements of dependency. If a question concerns how the biological model explains maintenance of smoking, material on anything else would not be creditworthy.

Evaluation

- Clark et al. (2009) finds that gambling near misses are misperceived as special events, encouraging gambling to continue. Brain activity is heightened in the striatum and insula cortex, areas that receive input from dopamine and which have been linked to other forms of addiction. This suggests that cognitive distortions, reinforcements and biological factors may all be involved in gambling dependency.
- The fact that dopamine is linked to dependency may lead to the manufacture of drugs acting upon dopamine production, which could reduce not only gambling dependency but other forms of addictive behaviour too.
- Kim and Grant (2001) find the drug naltrexone, which acts upon dopamine production, to be successful in reducing compulsions to gamble, lending support for a biological explanation but also demonstrating how such explanations can lead to effective practical applications.
- Paul (2008) reports that 20% of teenage gambling addicts contemplate suicide, demonstrating the pressing need for valid explanations of the condition in order for effective treatments to be developed.
- Children of chronic gamblers can experience improper emotional development, increasing their chances of becoming dependent gamblers. However, genetic and/or learning processes could also be factors in the process.
- Care must be taken when conducting research with dependent gamblers (or indeed any form of addiction) as ethical concerns of harm are heightened. It is arguable whether people with such pathological conditions can give informed consent.

Vulnerability to addiction

Specification content

- *Risk factors in the development of addiction, including stress, peers, age and personality*
- *Media influences on addictive behaviour*

The wording of the specification here indicates that the elements listed must be studied in a thorough fashion, as questions may be focused explicitly on any one of them. Focus of study should be on stress factors, peers, age and personality factors as specific risk factors in developing dependency, as well as media influences on addictive behaviour. Any relevant material is appropriate here.

Risk factors in the development of addiction

Several factors have been identified that affect vulnerability to addiction (i.e. each person's level of risk of becoming addicted). These factors can be applied to all forms of dependent behaviour.

stress factors biological and psychological stressors associated with the development of dependency behaviours

peers persons of equal status with influence on the development of dependency behaviours

personality factors characteristics associated with dependency behaviours

vulnerability to addiction the degree of susceptibility individuals have to dependency

Stress

More social stressors, such as poor housing and economic deprivation, tend to be found in urban environments, which are more associated with vulnerability to addiction. Increased stress levels correlate positively with increased vulnerability to dependency behaviours, usually as a way of trying to deal with the stress. Individuals who have a personality that is sensitive and negatively affected by stress are more vulnerable. Increased stressors are also associated with attempting to quit and maintaining quitting behaviour, which therefore can be responsible for relapses into dependency.

Increased stress can also be experienced through having a dependency, for example strained social relationships and the financial cost of dependency.

Research

- **Piazza et al. (1989)** found that rats repeatedly subjected to stress and given amphetamines showed increased activity in the dopamine neural system through behavioural sensitisation and became more disposed to self-administer amphetamines, which suggests stress affects drug-taking through physical affects upon neurobiology.
- **Cleck and Bendy (2008)** found an association between dependency behaviours and exposure to chronic, stressful life events such as sexual abuse. Also, the greater and longer the stressful life events, the more likely it was that dependencies would develop. Stressful events were also linked to increased drug usage and relapse into dependency, all of which suggests an influential role for stress in determining vulnerability to addiction.

Evaluation

- The high levels of drug usage in urban environments, where more stressors are found, may be a result of the heightened availability of drugs in such areas rather than of heightened stress.
- Much research into stress and addiction is done on animals, for ethical reasons, but findings may not be generalisable to humans, as the physiology of animals is often different from that of humans.

Peers

Peer pressure can be especially influential during adolescence if peers have positive attitudes towards dependency behaviours and thrill-seeking, and many individuals begin and maintain dependency behaviours due to peer influences. Individuals conform via normative social influence to peer pressure in order to be accepted, with dependency behaviours being adopted as 'in-group' norms. Peer pressure is also a form of operant conditioning and social learning, as peers reinforce dependency behaviours through praise and acceptance, as well as modelling addictive behaviours to be observed and imitated.

Examiner tip

The specification lists four risk factors in the development of addiction (stress, peers, age and personality) but take care when answering questions that you address the correct number of factors. For example, if a question asks for two factors, offering more will not gain extra credit but will waste valuable time better spent on another question.

- **Sussman and Ames (2001)** found peer usage of drugs was a strong indicator of drug use in adolescents, with deviant peers modelling and providing drugs, demonstrating the role that peers play in determining vulnerability levels.
- **Wagner and Anthony (2002)** found cannabis smokers were more likely to progress to cocaine usage if they were in peer groups that facilitated opportunities for new drug experiences, showing how peer groups can act as a 'gateway' to other dependencies.

Evaluation

- Peer influence should not be considered in isolation but in conjunction with other social contexts such as stress levels and personality, as they all combine to determine overall vulnerability levels.
- Leshner (1998) argued that peer groups can influence relapses into dependency, as recovered addicts tend to return to their old peer groups after leaving treatment clinics.

Age

Adolescence is the prime time for initiating dependency behaviours and, the earlier the onset, the reduced probability there is of individuals quitting, and the greater the possibility of relapsing after quitting. Early onset of dependency behaviour is also related to increased vulnerability to developing other dependencies.

Old age is also associated with increased vulnerability to addiction, with retirement often being a gateway to developing dependencies, through loss of status and also the increased stresses of old age such as boredom and the death of loved ones.

- **Health Canada Youth Smoking Survey (2006)** found early onset smokers were more likely to drink alcohol, binge drink and smoke cannabis, which suggests that early onset smoking acts as a gateway to other legal and illegal drug use.
- **Helfer (2006)** found a large increase in painkiller and tranquilliser usage in individuals between 55 and 64 years of age and that 46% of 75-year-old men drank every day, compared with only 6% of 25–34-year-olds, which highlights how old age is a time of increased risk of vulnerability to dependency behaviours.

Evaluation

- Research suggests public health initiatives would be more effective if targeted at the specific age groups identified as being more vulnerable to dependency.
- Dependency in old age is difficult to study, as older people are often reluctant to discuss such matters and their dependency behaviours are often much less visible than those in younger addicts. The media also tend to highlight dependency behaviour in the young and ignore such tendencies in the elderly.

Personality

Neurotic personality types characterised by moodiness, irritability and anxiety, and psychopathic personality types characterised by aggressiveness, emotional coldness and impulsiveness have been found to be more vulnerable to addiction, as substance abuse helps to reduce the effects of everyday stressors that affect psychologically fitter people less.

Although defective personality seems to increase vulnerability to dependency, research does not support the idea of a specific addictive personality type, though common personality characteristics such as a desire for immediate gratification, not valuing achievement, and high-levels of perceived stress are associated with increased vulnerability.

Knowledge check 13
Summarise how risk factors can affect vulnerability to addiction.

Research

- **Gossop and Eysenck (1980)** found that alcoholics had higher levels of neurotic characteristics associated with anxiety and depression than non-alcoholics, suggesting personality to be linked to increased vulnerability.
- **Chien et al. (1964)** found that low self-esteem, learned helplessness, passivity and a negative outlook on life were evident among ghetto addicts, suggesting a personality link to increased vulnerability to addiction.

Evaluation

- The idea that personality is associated with vulnerability to dependency is strengthened by the fact that individuals who overcome one dependency often develop a new one, for example abstaining from drugs, but then becoming an alcoholic.
- The idea that personality is associated with vulnerability to dependency is further strengthened by the fact that many recovered addicts develop strong behavioural compulsions towards other activities not seen as harmfully addictive, for example recovered addicts becoming obsessed with religion.

Media influences on addictive behaviour

Research has examined the extent to which the media affect addictive behaviours and the varying influences they exert on different age groups, with the focus mainly on the social learning effects, many of which are seen as presenting enhanced opportunities for the development of dependency behaviours. Another aspect of this study area is that of addictions to particular forms of media, creating a physiological dependence on social media and user-generated content. Research indicates this to be a growing problem due to the ever-increasing role of media in people's lives, such as the internet and television channels. The media can also affect people's conceptions through the nature of the content they offer, often in an invalid manner, such as the misrepresentation of addiction risks.

media public formats of communication that can influence dependency behaviours

Research

- **Kimberley (2006)** found social media to be extremely addictive in themselves, leading to increased usage to sustain 'highs' and increased anxiety without periodic access. Even relatively minor exposure can create physical and psychological dependence, suggesting social media addiction (SMA) to be a real and troublesome condition.
- **Roberts et al. (2002)** found that, contrary to popular belief, drug taking in music videos was fairly uncommon and portrayed the behaviour in a neutral manner. However, such portrayals could actually increase drug usage by depicting it as usual and commonplace.
- **The National Pain Foundation (NPF) (2008)** found that the media confuse people with misinformation on issues surrounding the addictive properties of pain-killing drugs, leading to chronic under-treatment of pain. Contrary to media portrayal, addiction is not a predictable side effect of narcotics, but may be a negative reaction by people with a genetic predisposition, and psychological vulnerability, to dependency.
- **Walther (1999)** reported on the increase in communication addiction disorder (CAD), where the disinhibition of the internet makes it attractive to potential addicts who have problems in establishing and maintaining normal social relationships. CAD creates serious disturbances in psychosocial functioning and an individual's ability to maintain positive work practices.
- **Charlton (1986)** found that viewing cigarette advertisements made children associate smoking with looking grown up and having confidence, showing the effects media can have upon addictive behaviours.
- **Gunsekera et al. (2005)** found drug taking in films to be portrayed in a positive fashion with little reference to possible negative consequences, suggesting that the media can influence dependency behaviour.

Examiner tip

As well as focusing on how the media influence addictive behaviour, it would also be creditworthy to comment on how media themselves are addictive, as there are many recent research studies in this area to draw upon, such as those focusing on social media addiction, for example, becoming addicted to e-mailing, texting or social network sites.

Evaluation

- The Centre for Addiction Recovery has developed the internet addiction test so that people can assess if they are at risk of developing social media addiction, demonstrating how psychological methodology can be used in a practical manner.
- The fact that people are affected differently by exposure to media sources suggests there may be individual differences in vulnerability to SMA and these may be linked to genetic factors.
- Farber (2007) reports that SMA is an increasing problem at work, with many employees feeling a constant need to access social media sites to the point of addiction. This suggests that such behaviour can seriously affect performance and damage output.
- The media can be seen to have both positive influences on addictive behaviours, such as the use of positive role models and education, as well as negative ones, such as negative role models, misinformation and addictions to media formats themselves.
- There is a danger that addicts can be demonised through media-created moral panics, seriously affecting the chances of addicts either receiving adequate social support to help them abstain, or seeking treatment in the first place.

- Media sources have proven especially influential with young children, who also tend not to question their credibility. This suggests that there should be an embargo on broadcasting programmes with content pertaining to addictive practices until after children's bedtime.
- The impact of media on addictive behaviour is hard to assess, as research tends to display correlations, which do not show cause-and-effect relationships. It is also possible that there are other variables at play.

Knowledge check 14

How can media influence addictive behaviour?

Reducing addictive behaviour

Specification content

- *The theory of planned behaviour as a model for addiction prevention*
- *Types of intervention and their effectiveness, including biological, psychological and public health interventions*

The specification here centres on the theory of planned behaviour, which must be covered thoroughly as it may feature directly in examination questions. Similarly, all the types of intervention listed and their effectiveness must be studied, as they too can be included as a specific requirement of examination questions.

Models of prevention

Theory of planned behaviour (TPB): Ajzen (1988)

The **theory of planned behaviour (TPB)** came out of the earlier theory of reasoned action (TRA), which saw dependency behaviours, and attempts to refrain from them, as due to decision making and factors that support decision making. TPB adds a new component, where addicts must be confident that their skills and resources are sufficient for them to abstain if they are to succeed in quitting. Overall the model has several components.

Theory of planned behaviour (TPB) an explanation of the factors that influence dependency behaviours

- **Behavioural beliefs** — linking the behaviour of interest to expected outcomes and comprising the subjective probability that behaviour will produce a given response. Behavioural beliefs determine the prevailing **attitude towards a behaviour**, the degree to which performance of such behaviour is positively or negatively valued.
- **Normative beliefs** — the perceived behavioural expectations of the relevant social group. They combine with an individual's level of motivation to determine the prevailing **subjective norm**, the perceived social pressure to be involved or not in the behaviour.
- **Control beliefs** — the perceived presence of factors that may help or hinder the performance of behaviour. They are seen as determining **perceived behavioural control**, referring to people's belief in their ability to perform a given behaviour. To the degree that it is an accurate measurement of actual behavioural control, perceived behavioural control can, along with **intention**, be used to predict behaviour (intention being a measure of an individual's willingness to perform a behaviour).

Examiner tip

Questions on TPB will focus on the model's ability to explain addiction prevention, so take care when learning and revising the model to concentrate specifically on this requirement, as merely presenting a general outline and evaluation of the model, without linking it to addiction prevention, will gain little credit.

TPB therefore allows consideration of an individual's reasons for continuing with dependency behaviours and their personal belief in their resolve to abstain. These are seen as important in the resolution to abstain and in resisting withdrawal effects and cravings. For this to succeed, a person's perceived behavioural control must be such as to lead them to believe they can overcome all problems (e.g. an alcoholic must be convinced that they will not buy alcohol or go to pubs, or accept drinks from others). The more a person believes that they have such behavioural control, the more the model predicts success in abstaining. The harder abstention is perceived to be, the more persistent they will be in attempting to quit.

Research

- **McMillan et al. (2005)** used TPB to investigate factors underlying smoking intentions and later smoking behaviour in school children. The theory produced good predictions of intentions, attitude, subjective norms and perceived behavioural control, though intentions did not fully predict the subjective norm–behaviour relationship, lending a degree of support to the model.
- **Oh and Hsu (2001)** used a questionnaire to assess gamblers' previous gambling behaviour, their social norms, attitudes, perceived behavioural control (like perceived gambling skills and levels of self-control) along with behavioural intentions. A positive correlation was found between their attitudes and behavioural intentions and actual behaviour, supporting the model.
- **Walsh and White (2007)** asked 252 university students to complete two questionnaires about high-level mobile phone use. The first measured TPB constructs of attitude, subjective norms and perceived behavioural control, and the second measured actual mobile phone use the previous week. Support for TPB was found in prediction of intentions and behaviour, though self-identity processes were also an influence.
- **Walker et al. (2006)** used interviews to assess whether TPB could explain gambling behaviour. Although some attitudes and norms were seen to be important, controllability was not an important factor for many participants in determining intention. Intention was found to be an important predictive factor, indicating some support for the model.

Knowledge check 15

Explain TPB as a model of addiction prevention.

Evaluation

- The model assumes behaviours are conscious, reasoned and planned, which may not always be the case with addicts.
- As with TRA, TPB may be reliant on invalid evidence, as research tends to rely on self-reports, which may be subject to social desirability (e.g. addicts playing down their degree of dependency) or because addicts may not be aware of the true extent of their dependency.
- Research indicates levels of perceived control differing between addicts and non-addicts. Goodwin (2005) found that chronic gamblers were more over-confident and showed greater acceptance of bets, indicating less influence of control.
- The model has a practical application in that health practitioners can use it to tailor treatment processes to individual needs.
- Although contributing greatly to our understanding of addiction, the lack of universal research support suggests further explanations are required if prevention treatments are to increase their successfulness.

Types of intervention and their effectiveness

Biological interventions

- **Detoxification programmes** — these involve gradual or instant abstention and often use antagonistic drugs, which block neurotransmitter receptors so that synaptic transmission is prevented, thus reducing withdrawal effects. Alternatively drugs can be used to address dependency directly.
- **Drug maintenance therapy** — this involves substitute drugs (e.g. methadone for heroin addicts which produces less of a high and is taken orally). This therapy does not involve contextual cues, like needles and pipes. Antagonistic and agonistic drugs can be used (see below).
  - **Antagonistic drugs** lessen or eliminate the effects of neurotransmitters by blocking cellular activity, altering the effects of addictive drugs. For example Buprenorphine is an antagonist used to reverse morphine addiction.
  - **Agonistic drugs** are site-specific drugs triggering cellular activity. As many drugs act upon dopamine levels to produce a 'high', dopamine agonists, such as Disulfiram, which reduces cocaine dependency by elevating dopamine levels, are used. In addition these drugs often lessen withdrawal symptoms by producing more dopamine in the brain.
- **Nicotine replacement therapy** — although nicotine is addictive, it is the other components of cigarettes, such as tar, that are dangerous. Therefore, nicotine is administered by means other than smoking, like patches or gum.

> **biological interventions** therapeutic methods of abstention from dependency behaviours, based upon physiological means

Research

- **Kosten et al. (2002)** evaluated the ability of a range of dopamine agonists to address addiction. Some indirect agonists, like Selegiline, proved useful in combating alcohol and cocaine dependence, with an indication that partial agonists and subtypes of dopamine receptors, like D3, may also be useful. This suggests that further research is required to identify which specific agonists combat which specific dependencies.
- **Moore et al. (2009)** assessed the effectiveness of a range of nicotine replacement therapies and found them to be an effective intervention therapy in achieving sustained abstinence for smokers who cannot or will not attempt immediate abstinence.
- **Warren et al. (2005)** assessed the effectiveness of methadone as a treatment for heroin addiction among 900 prisoners. Inmates who received methadone used heroin on an average of 15.24 days a year compared with 99.96 days a year for inmates not receiving methadone, showing methadone treatment to be extremely effective.

> **Examiner tip**
> Questions can be worth varying numbers of marks, so it is worthwhile practising writing shorter and longer versions of answers. For example, a question requiring an outline of biological interventions could be worth 4 marks for the description (requiring the shorter version) or 8 marks (therefore requiring the longer answer with more content and depth).

Evaluation

- Much research evidence comes from trials utilising behavioural support and monitoring and it is therefore unclear whether such therapies would be effective without regular contact.
- Drugs used to combat addictions can have serious side effects. Varenicline, used to treat smoking dependency, can result in depression and suicide, although withdrawal symptoms may contribute too.

- Methadone, an agonist often used to treat heroin addiction, has been associated with psychiatric disorders like depression. Trauer (2008) finds that those on methadone maintenance are ten times more likely to have a psychiatric disorder than the general population. However, Nunes et al. (1991) finds that treatment with imipramine reduces depression in 53% of such patients.

Psychological interventions

psychological interventions
therapeutic methods of abstention from dependency behaviours based upon non-physiological means

- **Cognitive therapies** attempt to forge trusting relationships with clients, taking an active, focused approach to identify and deconstruct false beliefs, reduce craving and help establish control over addictive behaviours. Triggers are identified and strategies developed that increase willpower, so that self-control becomes greater than the strength of the craving. Increased control is developed in therapy by artificially creating situations that produce cravings and developing methods of resistance like rational explanations to address false beliefs.

  Another cognitive-based strategy is cognitive–behavioural therapy (CBT), where the aim is to affect how an addict thinks about their dependency. Behavioural self-control training, enabling an addict to realise when they are at risk, is combined with coping skills such as relaxation techniques, to help resist temptation.
- **Aversion therapy** is a behaviourist treatment based on classical conditioning, where a negative effect is paired with the addictive substance so that the two become associated.
- **Operant conditioning** is another behaviourist treatment, based on voluntary behaviours. Reinforcement (e.g. being allowed visits, access to the internet etc.) is experienced each time an addict stays drug free for a target period. **Token economies** utilise operant conditioning and can be used in therapeutic communities, where non-addictive behaviour is rewarded with tokens that can be exchanged for desirable goods.

Research

- **Higgins et al. (1994)** found that 75% of cocaine addicts using operant conditioning in the form of token economies completed a drug rehabilitation course, compared with 40% using psychotherapy.
- **Carroll et al. (2008)** studied 77 individuals seeking treatment for substance abuse and found that those assigned to CBT produced more negative urine samples and longer periods of abstinence, suggesting that CBT is an effective method of treating substance abuse.
- **O'Farrel et al. (1985)** found that aversion therapy using the drug antabuse was successful in treating male alcoholics when combined with behavioural marital therapy, supporting the use of aversion therapy.
- **Williams and Connolly (2006)** found that cognitive interventions could change thinking, but not necessarily addictive behaviour, in chronic gamblers. However, **Floyd et al. (2006)** found that cognitive interventions when combined with a behavioural component to form CBT were an effective method of addressing gambling addiction.

Evaluation

- Behavioural treatments often have short-term, but not long-term, success in addressing addictions, possibly because they are addressing the effects of dependency rather than its causes.
- CBT is a relatively brief treatment and thus well suited to the resource capabilities of most clinical programmes and it can be tailored to many individuals' circumstances and situations. Its effects are long lasting and can even address the dependencies of severely addicted addicts.
- There is not much evidence that psychodynamic therapies can address addictions, but when used alongside other forms of treatment they may be effective. Woody et al. (1990) finds that a combination of methadone treatment and psychotherapy benefits the recovery of abstaining opiate addicts.

Public health interventions

- **Legislation and policing** — many attempts to influence addictive behaviours through legislation have been attempted and policing bodies have been utilised to try to enforce such legislation. Such policies can often, as with drinking and smoking, be aimed at specific age groups. However, although making drugs illegal may prevent some usage it can also increase the criminality associated with them, creating health issues such as disease risks and incidents of over-dosing/poisoning. The ban on smoking in public buildings has merely led to an increase in people smoking in outdoor areas and attempts in various countries at various times to ban such activities as gambling and drinking have served only to drive them underground and create significant criminal activity around their provision.
- **Health promotion** — can occur in various ways with varying degrees of success.
- **Social inoculation** — attempts to strengthen people's attempts to resist temptation and persuasion to take up addictive activities by providing counterarguments as an inoculation defence against such attempts and also by providing supportive defence statements that reinforce beliefs people already hold.
- **Fear arousal** — often used in health campaigns to try to strengthen the persuasiveness of arguments against addictive practices.
- **Targeting risk groups** — based on the idea that health promotion campaigns will be more successful if they are specifically aimed at those who are most at risk and will therefore benefit most from them, making the campaigns more cost effective.

Research

- **McGuire (1964)** found that the use of **inoculation defence** in the form of counterarguments and **supportive defence** in the form of strengthening statements helped individuals to resist temptation and persuasion to indulge in addictive behaviours.
- **Lemstra et al. (2008)** compared smoking rates in Saskatoon, a Canadian city where a smoking ban was introduced, with Saskatchewan, which had no smoking ban. The smoking rate in Saskatoon was reduced from 24% to 18% in a 2-year period, while remaining at 34% in Saskatchewan, suggesting that legislation can be effective.

Examiner tip

When answering questions on interventions and their effectiveness, make use of research studies, as they provide descriptive and evaluative content. Outlining aims, procedures and findings earns credit as description, while commenting on what research findings suggest in terms of support for explanations/theories gains credit as evaluation. Research studies often suggest practical applications, regarded as an additional source of evaluation.

public health interventions communal campaigns that seek to reduce and protect against dependency behaviours

- **Quist-Paulsen and Gallefoss (2007)** studied the effect of fear arousal on smoking levels in Norwegian cardiac patients. It was found that those subjected to fear arousal were more able to give up smoking and avoid relapse over a 12-month period, suggesting that such a strategy is effective.
- **Conrod et al. (2004)** introduced the 'preventure programme' to identify 13–16-year-olds at risk of developing substance abuse. Resources were then targeted at those identified, focusing on risk factors for early-onset abuse. From 2,696 participants, 423 were identified as at risk and subsequent targeting of resources at these individuals was deemed to show successful outcomes.

Knowledge check 16

How do biological, psychological and public health interventions work and how effective are they?

Evaluation

- Health campaigns seem to work best when based on models of behaviour change like TPB.
- Smoking bans tend to reduce cigarette sales, but may make chronic smokers more determined not to quit.
- It is often difficult to evaluate legislative attempts to curb addictive practices, as criminalising the activity makes it difficult to assess how many users there are.
- Identifying risk groups can be a cost-effective strategy as it targets resources at those who might benefit most from them.

Summary

- The biological approach perceives addiction as a physiologically controlled pattern of behaviour, while the cognitive approach sees it as involving distorted thinking relating to dysfunctional beliefs. Alternatively, the learning approach sees it as involving environmental interactions based on classical and operant conditioning, as well as social learning theory.
- The biological, cognitive and learning approaches can all help explain smoking and gambling in relation to initiation, maintenance and relapse.
- Risk factors increasing vulnerability to addiction include, stress, peers, age and personality. These can have an individual influence or work in combination with each other.
- The media influence addictive behaviour through social learning theory and misrepresentations of addiction risk, while being addictive themselves.

- TPB is an explanation of the factors influencing dependent behaviour, consisting of behavioural, normative and control beliefs, and perceives personal beliefs concerning the resolve to abstain as the main factor in quitting dependency behaviours.
- Biological interventions consist of physiological means of abstention such as drugs, which are effective but incur side effects.
- Psychological interventions involve non-physiological therapeutic methods of abstention such as CBT and aversion therapy, both showing high levels of effectiveness.
- Public health interventions include legislation, health promotion, social inoculation, fear arousal and the targeting of risk groups.

Anomalistic psychology

The study of anomalous experience

Specification content

- *Pseudoscience and the scientific status of parapsychology*
- *Methodological issues related to the study of paranormal cognition (ESP, including Ganzfeld) and paranormal action (psychokinesis)*

The specification first focuses on pseudoscience and the scientific status of parapsychology, with students needing to be able both to outline and to evaluate these areas, before focusing attention specifically upon ESP, which must include the Ganzfeld technique and studies, and psychokinesis. As these are explicitly named, specific questions could be asked about them.

Pseudoscience

Pseudoscience means 'false science' and refers to so-called sciences and scientific practices that have little or no scientific basis, such as astrology. Examples of pseudoscience, and **scientific fraud**, have occurred in mainstream psychology but there is more scope for these approaches within the study of **anomalistic psychology**. There are critics, however, who claim that the term 'pseudoscience' has been abused as a weapon with which to attack innovation.

Pseudoscience is potentially dangerous as it could lead to the acceptance of 'facts' that are not true, and practical applications based on such falsehoods could have damaging implications for society. For example, eugenics is a pseudoscience that stated intelligence was genetically transmitted. This unproven belief led to the forced sterilisation of people of low IQ, generally black people with little schooling. In essence it was nothing more than racism dressed up in pseudoscientific terms and did immense harm to society and to the reputation of psychology.

Telepathy

Telepathy is a belief in communication through means other than the senses. In the 1950s a London University mathematician called Samuel Soal claimed to have convincing evidence of telepathy with a special subject, Basil Shackleton. Zener cards were used, which have five symbols repeated over 25 cards. Soal looked at each card and Shackleton then reported what the researcher was seeing. The participant was good; odds were estimated at 1,035 to 1 that the effect was due to chance. The evidence seemed convincing and a whole generation of researchers believed in Soal's findings. It was over 20 years before Markwick (1978) showed that Soal had cheated by reanalysing the original results and finding that false data had been added which, when removed, reduced Soal's findings to within chance levels.

pseudoscience a body of knowledge that is proposed as scientific, but which fails to comply with accepted scientific method

scientific fraud fabrication, falsification and plagiarism of research data

anomalistic psychology the study of extraordinary phenomena of behaviour and experience

telepathy communication through means other than by sensory data

The scientific status of parapsychology

Parapsychology (PP) has at times had problems with deliberate fraud (see telepathy, page 45), but the debate with PP is generally more to do with whether anomalistic psychology can ever have scientific status and its phenomena be studied in a scientific manner.

PP was a term introduced in the 1930s to refer to the scientific study of anomalistic phenomena. Science generally deals only with sensory experiences but PP is based on the idea that phenomena based on exchanges of information that go beyond sensory experience can also be studied in a scientific manner.

PP has had three phases:

(1) Spiritualism — concerning a search for the souls of the dead
(2) Psychical research — concerning the pursuit of ghosts, possession, telepathy etc.
(3) Parapsychology — concerning a laboratory-based, scientifically rigorous examination of anomalistic phenomena in an unbiased and objective fashion

Parapsychology as science

The world of PP is ever-shrinking as, when anomalistic phenomena such as hallucinations become understood in a scientifically explicable manner, then they are no longer considered paranormal. This suggests that PP can study only phenomena that lie outside the scope of normal scientific understanding. This creates a fundamental argument, as sceptics believe that paranormal phenomena are scientifically impossible and thus PP and its research methods can never be scientifically legitimate (especially as many practitioners have been proven to be frauds), while others argue that science should never reject the possibility of anomalistic phenomena being shown one day to be true. Indeed, many parapsychologists argue that evidence for the existence of such phenomena has already been provided that has withstood far more rigorous scientific scrutiny than many non-parapsychological phenomena that are accepted as true.

Knowledge check 17

Is parapsychology a science or a pseudoscience?

Evaluation

- Song (2006) believes that, if the scientific community label as pseudoscience theories they do not know or understand, then science will be restrained from making innovations and scientific progress.
- Ren (2007) believes that science should not be based solely upon repeatable experiments. However, Zhao argues that science is not an over-conservative discipline but accepts only theories offering persuasive evidence.
- Blackmore (2001) claims that pseudoscience in psychology exists because of a popular belief in the existence of a consciousness seen as the controlling mechanism of the mind and there exists, therefore, a desire to find the 'power of consciousness'.
- Mahner (2007) argues that, since science is our most reliable source of knowledge, we need to distinguish scientific knowledge from its lookalikes.

- Science is a process where errors are isolated and cut out one by one, with hypotheses framed in such a way that it is possible to disprove them. A succession of better, alternative, hypotheses is created, leading to verisimilitude (closeness to the truth). However, pseudoscience does the opposite, as it proposes hypotheses that cannot be falsified through scientific means and does not encourage sceptical analysis.
- Instances of fraud and the high level of scepticism have led to the development of research procedures in PP that are probably the most rigorous in psychology, including automated target selection and result recording, predetermined number of trials and independent assessment.
- Pseudoscience dresses itself up in scientific terminology and mirrors scientific practice because it wishes to acquire the high-status and acceptability science holds in society.
- It is important to have a demarcation between science and pseudoscience, as the acceptance of pseudoscientific beliefs and practices could lead to inefficient and dangerous practices in health care, environmental policy, science education and courts of law.
- Sagan (2010) argues that pseudoscience hinders proper science, as it offers easy answers, avoids difficult scrutiny and champions impossible, but desirable, practices, like that of astrology. Pseudoscience pretends to be scientific but is not based on fully established facts, ignores contrary evidence, avoids contact with reality and is accepted too easily by gullible people. He believes pseudoscience continues to be popular as it fulfils powerful emotional needs that science leaves unfulfilled, satisfies spiritual hunger, promises cures for disease and the existence of an afterlife and convinces humans of their supreme importance in the universe.
- Some pseudosciences, like homeopathy, swing between being anti-science and claiming they represent 'good' science.

Methodological issues related to the study of paranormal cognition

Ganzfeld studies

Metzger introduced the Ganzfeld (entire field) technique in the 1930s. The technique uses unpatterned sensory stimulation to produce an effect similar to sensory deprivation. Honorton (1974) developed the technique to assess extrasensory perception (ESP) and it is now the main tool of parapsychological research.

In Ganzfeld studies, a **receiver** relaxes in a room for half an hour with halved table-tennis balls on their eyes, receiving white noise through headphones, creating a mild sense of sensory deprivation. A **sender** tries to communicate mentally a randomly chosen object, with the receiver describing mental communications they feel they have received. During the judging procedure, the receiver, now out of the Ganzfeld state, has four possible targets and chooses the one best fitting the images experienced. This gives a 25% chance of the correct response. Some claim results

Ganzfeld studies
a research methodology of forced-choice pre-recognition target identification

gained go beyond this figure, but critics claim that such research is inconclusive and cannot be taken as evidence for the existence of ESP.

Research

- **Honorton (1982)** presented the results of 88 Ganzfeld studies, claiming 1,008 correct answers out of a possible 3,145 (32%). This is outside the boundaries of chance, and supports the existence of ESP.
- **Hyman (1985)** and **Honorton** produced independent meta-analyses of Ganzfeld data and although Honorton claimed support for ESP Hyman did not, claiming the experimental procedures were neither rigorous enough nor correctly analysed statistically, citing flaws in the randomisation of targets and the judging procedure as well as insufficient documentation. Honorton claimed that Hyman assessed too few data to perform a proper factor analysis.
- **Hyman and Honorton (1986)** issued a joint communiqué agreeing that the results were not due to chance or biased reporting and agreeing a need for replication performed under more stringent, mutually agreed conditions. Honorton then conducted autoganzfeld experiments using computer-controlled tests with the receiver isolated in a soundproof, steel-walled, electromagnetically shielded room.
- **Honorton (1990)** reported 122 correct responses out of a possible 354 (34%) using the autoganzfeld technique, a statistically significant result. Hyman stated that the results could only be accepted if confirmed by independent investigators.
- **Milton and Wiseman (1999)** carried out a meta-analysis of 30 independent studies and found no significant result. This was criticised for using non-standard methods (for instance musical rather than visual targets).
- **Bem and Palmer (2001)** redid the meta-analysis on studies using the standard procedure, with ten new additional studies, and found a significant result.
- **Blackmore (1987)** reported on a visit to the laboratory of Sargent, a leading parapsychologist, and criticised his Ganzfeld research practices. Sargent blamed random errors rather than deliberate fraud but retired from further research.

Evaluation

- There is a danger of demand characteristics occurring with the Ganzfeld technique (believers in paranormal experiences produce seemingly correct answers). Results from Ganzfeld studies tend to match the beliefs of the researcher.
- Hyman (1995) claims that results will remain meaningless until an explanation of the process behind them is outlined and validated.
- Wiseman (1999) claims that not all Honorton's autoganzfeld studies were conducted under rigorous conditions.
- The use of the Ganzfeld technique has led to the introduction of more rigorously controlled, unbiased research techniques.

Examiner tip

The specification here is concentrated on methodological issues, so it is perfectly acceptable, and indeed good practice, to make explicit points about methodology, for instance, the role of rigorous investigative procedures in Ganzfeld experiments and the role of researcher bias in determining results.

Knowledge check 18

Does research support the existence of ESP?

AQA(A) A2 Psychology

Studies of psychokinesis

Psychokinesis (PK) is the process of moving or otherwise affecting physical objects through the mind only, with no physical contact. The most famous practitioner is Uri Geller, a celebrity who supposedly uses PK to bend spoons. This is an example of **macro-PK**, which has an obvious effect. **Micro-PK** involves small effects on systems of probability, like throwing dice. Claims have been made by psychics to be able to effect levitation, move objects and control weather patterns.

psychokinesis a technique of mind over matter through invisible means

Research

- **Mishlove (2000)** reported to the Institute of Parascience in 1976 on Ted Owens, a man with extraordinary supernatural powers, verifying his claims to have demonstrated PK. Others testified to his power to influence the weather. However, Owens's credibility seems dubious as he also claimed to be the supreme Earth ambassador for UFO intelligences, having been operated on by them to allow communication, the first such person since Moses. Mishlove admitted that Owens had mental problems, but claimed, 'we have much to learn about the interface between mental illness and the paranormal'.

- **Radin and Ferrari (1991)** reported on 148 dice-rolling experiments performed by 52 investigators between 1934 and 1987 involving 2.6 million dice throws. A meta-analysis was conducted and a small but significant result was found. However, **Hansel (1989)** reported that when criteria necessary for a conclusive PK test were applied (having two researchers, true randomisation of targets and independent recorders) none of the tests produced evidence for PK that could be regarded as conclusive.

- **Schmidt (1970)** asked participants to observe a circle of nine lamps and when one was lit to try to move it mentally in a certain direction. It was found that some participants appeared able to exert an influence, suggesting support for the existence of PK.

- **Schmidt (1976)** had similar success when asking participants to influence clicks on a cassette tape generated randomly by a radioactive source. They could be made stronger or weaker by mental effort, producing convincing evidence for the existence of PK.

- **Stevens (1999)** used the internet to research PK and asked participants accessing a web page to try to control the paths of laser beams, finding more influence over the beams than in a control condition of no mental effort, supporting the notion of PK.

- **Benson et al. (2006)** asked three groups of Christians to pray for heart bypass surgery patients, with a control group of similar patients who were not prayed for. No significant differences in recovery rates were found, indeed the prayed-for group had more complications. This suggests that prayer has no effect, though members of the control group may have been prayed for by friends and family.

Examiner tip
Research studies of telekinesis (and ESP) can provide both descriptive and evaluative content. Outlining aims, procedures and findings earns credit as description, while commenting on methodological issues and what research findings suggest in terms of support for the existence of paranormal cognition gains credit as evaluation.

Evaluation

- Magicians such as Randi have demonstrated the skills required for psychic processes, implying that other more natural processes are operating.
- Although there is evidence for the existence of PK, independent researchers cannot often replicate findings.
- Schmeidler and McConnell (1958) find that believers of psychic phenomena produce more supporting evidence on tests of paranormal abilities and therefore results for PK are explainable as due to participant and researcher bias.
- Weil (1974) argues that what we perceive is not necessarily what actually occurs, because beliefs affect perception and we see what we want or expect to see.
- There is a misconception that if a researcher is testing paranormal ability they must be measuring it. This is not necessarily true. They may merely be measuring the difference between chance predictions and actual outcome, with a bias towards the existence of PK emerging due to the fact that studies finding no significant results are never published.
- Radin (1997) believes that the insular nature of scientific disciplines hinders the acceptance of parapsychologists' work by other scientists.
- Randi (2003) argues that if PK exists then the question of why it is not used for human good (rather than merely bending spoons and so on) is raised.

Knowledge check 19

Does research evidence support the existence of PK?

coincidence a sequence of accidental events that is perceived as planned

probability judgements the reasoning associated with the calculation of the possibility of events occurring

superstition an irrational belief that an object, action or circumstance not logically related to a course of events can influence its outcome

magical thinking the belief that the mind can have a direct effect on the physical world

personality factors dispositional characteristics associated with beliefs in, and experience of, anomalous experience

Explanations for anomalous experience

Specification content

- *The role of coincidence and probability judgements in anomalous experience*
- *Explanations for superstitious behaviour and magical thinking*
- *Personality factors underlying anomalous experience*

Attention initially focuses on the role of coincidence and probability judgements in anomalous experience and, as these are explicitly listed, they may form direct questions. A working knowledge of explanations for superstitions and magical thinking is also required but, as no specific explanations are stated, all relevant ones would be creditworthy. There is a final requirement to study personality factors underlying anomalous experience, though, as no specific ones are listed, all relevant ones would again be creditworthy.

The role of coincidence and probability judgements in anomalous experience

Coincidence

A coincidence occurs when two unrelated events coincide. Although no obvious relationship exists, a belief in a relationship forms, creating a cognitive bias that one causes the other. This is offered as an explanation of how superstitions arise. The perception of coincidences leads to occult or paranormal claims, supporting the belief system of fatalism, where events are seen as predestined. Coincidences also happen due to shortcuts in information processing occurring as an attempt to simplify understanding.

Research

- **Falk (1982)** found that, when an extraordinary coincidence occurs, people commit the error of singling that event out and according it significant status, suggesting a bias in cognitive processing.
- **Falk (1989)** found that unlikely coincidences were considered more significant when they happen to us, suggesting an egocentric bias at play.
- **Zusne and Jones (1989)** calculated that 30,000 Americans each year would think of someone they knew five minutes before learning of their death, which illustrates how easy it would be to assume that what was actually a coincidence was a paranormal event.

Evaluation

- Chopra (2003) believes that the ancient Vedic philosophy that all events can be related to unseen prior causes or associations, no matter how vast or trivial, and that there is therefore no such thing as coincidence, is becoming accepted by scientists.
- Slovic et al. (1982) believe that, when unlikely events such as bizarre accidents happen, it serves to remind us of our own mortality.
- The calculation of coincidence is dependent on accurate memory of how many times, or how often, certain events have occurred in the past. As memory can be reconstructive, as well as subject to wishful thinking and suggestion, this may not actually occur, leading people to believe that paranormal events have taken place.

Probability judgements

People often miscalculate the probability of unrelated events occurring, believing instead that they are connected through some paranormal source. For example, the chances of something in a dream coming true out of all the things an individual dreams about is quite high and explainable as pure, unrelated coincidence, but many individuals will be convinced or prefer to believe that it is evidence of psychic forces at play.

The fact that belief in paranormal forces has increased suggests that people do not use logical reasoning or scientific evidence but look instead to media depictions of paranormal explanations and misperceptions of personal experience and other people's experiences as being evidence of anomalistic phenomena.

There are several cognitive factors involved in people's inabilities to calculate correct probability judgements and preferences for believing in paranormal events instead of coincidence:

Examiner tip
The wording of the specification is such that questions could be asked on either coincidence or probability judgements, or on both together (the situation is the same with explanations for superstitious behaviour and magical thinking). So it is a good idea when revising to practise different types of answer, so you are prepared for all eventualities.

Knowledge check 20

Why might people miscalculate coincidences and probability judgements?

(1) Intuitive thinking style — such individuals lack reasoning power and critical thinking ability so that evidence is not evaluated analytically.

(2) Cognitive illusions — such individuals are prone to believing in the paranormal, misperceiving probability and reading significance into random patterns.

(3) Illusion of control — such individuals tend to perceive random processes as being under personal control due to mastery and skill.

(4) Confirmatory bias — such individuals tend to ignore contrary evidence and focus instead on confirmatory evidence.

Research

- **Esgate and Groome** (2001) found that participants overestimated how big a group of people needs to be for there to be a 50:50 chance of two of them sharing a birthday (it's actually 23 people), illustrating how individuals can easily miscalculate and assume paranormal phenomena are occurring.
- **Paulus (1988)** reported that believers in the paranormal see dreams as being predictive, on the basis of an event in a dream and a future event coinciding, illustrating how some individuals miscalculate probabilities.
- **Blackmore and Troscianko (1985)** found believers in the paranormal were worse than non-believers in generating random numbers, which implies that believers in the paranormal are subject to cognitive illusions and thus misperceive probability.

Evaluation

- Research does not indicate where cognitive factors associated with misjudging the probability of paranormal events originate, so it is not known whether they are innate or learned from experience. Banziger (1983) found that students on a parapsychology course that emphasised scepticism became more sceptical in their thinking, which suggests that cognitive styles can be altered by experience, leading to a change in probability judgements.
- Individuals having differences in cognitive styles relating to detecting patterns in phenomena where none actually exist is explicable in evolutionary terms as a biological device to try to make sense of the world, which thus has a survival value.

Explanations for superstitious behaviour and magical thinking

Superstition

A superstition is an irrational belief that an object, action or circumstance not logically related to a course of events influences the outcome of those events. It is often linked to magical thinking and ritual behaviours if they are seen as magically affecting an outcome. Although superstitions can be obsessive, they are not seen as characteristics of obsessive–compulsive disorder.

The motivation behind superstitions is a desire for control and certainty, with individuals searching for a rule or explanation of why things happen. The creation of false certainties through superstition is regarded as better than having no certainty at all and this is especially so in situations where we want success, such as our football team winning.

Behaviourism explains superstitions through operant conditioning, either by positive reinforcement (where certain behaviours or objects become associated with pleasurable outcomes) or by negative reinforcement (where behaviours or objects become associated with reducing the anxiety levels associated with uncertainty).

Research

- **Skinner (1948)** found that pigeons adopted unique body movement superstitions, by learning to associate them with rewards of food pellets.
- **Lustberg (2004)** found superstitions among sportspeople to be beneficial, as they increased confidence, motivation and persistence, thus enhancing chances of winning.
- **Fluke et al. (2010)** found that superstitions help individuals to feel in control of uncertain situations, decrease feelings of helplessness, and are easier to rely on than using coping strategies, which suggests superstitions fulfil several functions.

Evaluation

- Vyse (2009) believes that superstitions provide people with the sense that they have done something to try to ensure they gain a desirable outcome.
- Foxman (2009) says superstitions create expectations that can be extremely powerful and suggestive, leading to biases to see them as true, but they can also have a negative influence by reinforcing maladaptive behaviours such as gambling.
- Superstitions help maintain psychological health, as they decrease anxiety levels while increasing confidence and self-assurance. They can also negatively affect psychological health through believers in superstitions seeing themselves as responsible for poor outcomes.

Magical thinking

Magical thinking sees all things as connected by paranormal forces and believes that special powers such as energy forces exist in things perceived as symbols, such as water possessing a purifying effect. Magical thinking proposes the **law of similarity**, where things and events that resemble each other are connected in a way that defies scientific explanation and investigation, as well as the **law of contagion**, where things that have been associated with each other retain their connection after separation, like the bones of dead saints retaining spiritual energy. Most religions contain elements of magical thinking, for example believing that dead saints can cure 'incurable' diseases.

Research

- **Rachman and Safran (1999)** reported on thought–action fusion, a type of magical thinking where intrusive thoughts are believed to have physical effects, such as some anorexics believing that merely thinking about food creates weight gain. Such findings could help clinicians to understand and treat eating disorders better.

> **Examiner tip**
> The specification is concentrated on 'explanations for superstitious behaviour and magical thinking' so, when creating evaluations, take care not to focus on other areas such as methodological issues, because this approach will gain little credit. Instead, evaluations should focus explicitly on explanations, for instance, their degree of research support.

- **Irwin (1994)** found that children who grew up with an alcoholic parent were more likely to indulge in magical thinking, which suggests that it has a coping function.
- **Bonser (1963)** reported that Mapuche Indians in Chile favoured taking red pills, as red was associated with exorcism, and they thus believed red pills could purge illness. This supports the magical thinking belief that psychic forces exist in things perceived as symbols.

Evaluation

- Magical thinking can be perceived as an attempt to find meaningful connections between things, thus serving to create a sense of certainty and control. This can be seen as an evolutionary device, as possessing a greater understanding of the world would bestow a survival value.
- A practical application of Bonser's research could be to manufacture pills in colours associated with different healing powers, such as blue pills for stress conditions, because blue is associated with calmness.
- Magical thinking could actually have a real effect at times, as a belief in something being so can increase the chances of its actually occurring. For example, a belief that prayer can cure sickness would give believers a positive outlook on recovering from illness, thus increasing their chances of getting better.

Knowledge check 21

Why might superstitious behaviour and magical thinking occur?

Personality factors underlying anomalous experience

Psychologists have found that neurotic characteristics of anxiety, moodiness and emotional instability are associated with a belief in the paranormal, which may occur because neurotics find paranormal phenomena a source of comfort, as they allow them to believe that they can understand and predict events, reducing their tendency to panic and be overemotional. Researchers have also found that extroverts are more likely to possess ESP abilities, possibly as they have lower natural levels of arousal in the reticular activating system (RAS) of the brain.

Early research suggested a relationship between external locus of control and belief in the paranormal as giving an illusion of control. However, subsequent research using specific measuring tools showed a link between external locus of control and superstition (suggesting a belief in fate) and an internal locus of control related to a belief in ESP (suggesting control by willpower).

Another personality characteristic, that of defensiveness, which involves a cognitive resistance to perceiving situations and information as threatening, has also been linked to anomalous experience. Individuals who demonstrate such defensive reactions tend to score lower for ESP than non-defensive individuals.

Examiner tip

Questions can be worth varying amounts of marks, so it is worthwhile practising writing shorter and longer versions of answers. For example, a question requiring an outline of personality factors underlying anomalous experience could be worth 4 marks for the description, therefore requiring the shorter version, or 8 marks, therefore requiring the longer answer with more content and depth.

Research
- **Tobayck and Milford (1983)** found a relationship between external locus of control and greater belief in paranormal phenomena, which suggests a belief in fate, an external factor outside an individual's control.
- **Davies and Kirkby (1985)** found a relationship between internal locus of control and a belief in ESP, which suggests a belief in control through willpower — an internal factor within an individual's control.
- **Wiseman and Watt (2004)** found, using personality questionnaires, that neuroticism positively correlated with a belief in the paranormal, suggesting a link with personality.

Knowledge check 22
In what ways is personality associated with a belief in the paranormal?

Evaluation
- The relationship between personality and anomalous beliefs is not a simple one, as different personality characteristics appear to be associated with different aspects of paranormal beliefs. For example, neuroticism is associated with beliefs in the paranormal, while extroversion is associated with psychic abilities such as ESP.
- It may be that extroverts demonstrate ESP abilities simply because they adapt to the novel social environment of the laboratory more quickly and are aroused, motivated and comfortable with being tested. Introverts may not show such abilities, as they do not engage with such scrutiny.
- Defensive individuals may score lower for ESP, as extrasensory information is initially perceived at an unconscious level, before being transformed to appear in the conscious arena, and defensive individuals may be resistant to this process.

Research into exceptional experience

Specification content
- *Psychological research into and explanations for psychic healing, near-death and out of body experiences, and psychic mediumship*

The specification focuses on three explicit areas of exceptional experience and examination questions could be directed at any of or all these. Students should be able to outline and evaluate each of these.

Psychic healing

There are many instances of people reporting psychic healing powers, often by 'therapeutic touch', known as the 'laying on of hands'. Other claims have been made for distance healing, where people are treated without physical contact and over large distances. Charismatic religious figures are often seen as possessing such a 'gift' and thus attain elevated status.

psychic healing the restoration of health through spiritual practices

Psychic healers sometimes use media such as crystals to 'tap into' bodily energy fields and sources, although much of the theory surrounding such ideas tends to be subjective and is not backed up with empirical evidence.

Research

- **Grad (1959)** studied Oskar Estabany, a cavalry officer who discovered his healing powers when treating army horses, finding that mice who had a portion of skin removed recovered faster if treated by Estabany. During his treatments, production of the enzyme trypsin was stimulated, suggesting a biological basis to psychic healing.
- **Krieger (1979)** found that haemoglobin levels were stimulated during Estabany's treatments of humans and stayed elevated for a year after the treatment, again implying a biological basis for his powers.
- **Ostrander and Schroeder (1970)** documented the abilities of Colonel Alexei Krivorotov, who placed his hands close to the patient's body and the patient would report a feeling of heat. However, no change in temperature could be found in either the healer's hands or the patient's skin, implying that any beneficial effect was the result of suggestive power or the placebo effect.
- **Braud and Schlitz (1988)** investigated distance healing, asking healers to focus attention on photographs of patients for 1-minute periods. The patients were unaware of this procedure, thus ruling out the possibility of a placebo or suggestive effect. During the 1-minute healing periods it was found that patients' galvanic skin responses (GSR), often associated with activity in the sympathetic nervous system, altered, suggesting a real biological influence.
- **West (1957)** reviewed the medical records of 11 cases of miracle cures occurring at the shrine of Lourdes and given official 'miraculous' status by the Catholic Church. The records were found to be disappointing as crucial information was missing, a conclusion similarly reached by magician James Randi, who examined the data at a later date. The 11 miracles cannot therefore be taken as irrefutable evidence for psychic healing, especially when the fact that at least 6 million people have visited Lourdes in search of miracle cures is taken into account.
- **Droscher (1971)** reported on the phenomenon of musical psychic healing, where vocal music is used to heal. He believed this occurred because humans can hear ultrasonic sounds within their heads and these ultrasonics combine with body chemistry to facilitate healing. However, the evidence to show how this would actually take place is lacking.

Evaluation

- Guinan (2004) reports, after an extensive review of scientific literature, that the Catholic Church's Medical Association has banned the practice of 'therapeutic touch'.
- Psychic healing may occur because it has some real biological effect, or it may just be a form of spontaneous recovery based on the presence of a caring person reducing a patient's anxieties and fears to facilitate healing, or a type of short-term recovery, possibly due to suggestion, or it may be the result of a placebo effect (where a fake treatment can improve a patient's condition simply because the person has the expectation it will be helpful).

Examiner tip

With the belief in exceptional experience topic, the specification focuses on explanations and research studies, so answers need to focus on the explicit requirements of questions. If a question concerns explanations and only research evidence is offered, few marks, if any, will be gained. Conversely, if a question asks about research studies, then that is what answers should focus on.

AQA(A) A2 Psychology

- The suspicion exists that many studies have not been rigorously controlled and therefore experimenter effects and demand characteristics have occurred. More stringent studies are required, especially of replications of earlier studies.
- One implication of finding support for psychic healing is that some people may be paying out large sums of money to fake practitioners, who also receive elevated status and respectability.
- Medical doctors are educated in how to heal and how such treatments work. Few, if any, psychic healers have prior medical training/knowledge, and the question of how they can heal without being familiar with the complexities of the human body arises. One suggestion is that psychic healing is a real phenomenon and that psychic healers are in some unconscious way able to help our bodies tap into natural bodily defences and healing resources.
- Mollica (2005) suggests that psychic healers are beneficial in dealing with the widespread trauma occurring after catastrophes, like the Asian tsunami. Patients treated by culturally familiar methods like psychic healing often benefit more than those treated only medically because they offer 'psychological first aid' that is neither intrusive nor anxiety creating.

Knowledge check 23
Explain what is meant by psychic healing.

Out-of-body and near-death experiences

The term out-of-body experience (OBE) developed as a more bias-free label than other terms (e.g. 'astral projection' or 'spirit walking'). OBEs generally involve a feeling of floating outside your body, or even being able to see your own body from an exterior place.

out-of-body-experience a vivid sensation of being outside one's physical being

OBEs occur as several subtypes: there are **parasomatic** OBEs, where an individual has another body other than their usual one, and **asomatic** OBEs, where an individual feels they have no body. A rare subtype occurs when an individual feels there is a connecting cord between bodies.

The majority of OBEs occur when in bed, suggesting a link to sleep and dream states. They can also occur due to drug usage, such as ketamine.

Some people who have experienced OBEs believe it was something that they willed themselves, while others report a sensation of being pulled involuntarily from their bodies, usually after a feeling of general paralysis. This suggests that OBEs may be occurring during a borderline stage between REM sleep and arousal when sleep paralysis occurs and dream images mix with usual sensory input.

OBEs can often be encountered by people having dangerous near-death experiences (NDEs).

near-death experiences sensations in which people who are near death, but survive, report being exterior to their body, and the circumstances surrounding it

Research
- **Blanke et al. (2005)** found that OBEs were simulated in participants with no history of OBEs by electrical stimulation of the right temporal-parietal brain area, suggesting a biological explanation.
- **Ehrsson et al. (2007)** found a way to simulate OBEs. Virtual reality goggles were used to con the brain into thinking the body was located elsewhere. Participants' real bodies were then touched and the visual illusion plus the feel of their real bodies being touched made volunteers sense that they had moved outside their physical bodies, suggesting that OBEs may be triggered by a mismatch between visual and tactile signals.

Questions on OBEs and NDEs are likely to focus on both together, as people who experience NDEs often report OBEs. Therefore the focus of answers should be on explaining why OBEs occur and why they should occur with NDEs. Research studies could be used to evaluate to what extent such explanations are valid.

- **Parnia et al. (2008)** began a 3-year investigation of near-death experiences in 1,500 heart attack survivors, the aim being to determine whether people with no heartbeat or brain activity could have verifiable OBEs.
- **Van Lommel et al. (2001)** researched the cases of 344 patients successfully resuscitated after suffering heart attacks. Of these, 18% reported having near-death experiences, including OBEs, during a period when they were clinically dead with little if any brain activity. It was concluded that continuity of consciousness is possible if the brain acts as a receiver for information generated from memory and consciousness existing independently of the brain.
- **Irwin (1985)** reported that OBEs occur with very low or very high arousal. **Green (1968)** found that 75% of participants experiencing an OBE had very low arousal as they were lying down when the episode occurred, while a substantial minority of cases happened during high arousal, such as a rock-climbing fall or childbirth.
- **Greyson (1997)** developed an experimental technique for investigating NDEs. During cardioverter-defibrillator implantations, doctors induce heart attacks to test the device and such an operation therefore carries with it a significant possibility of NDEs occurring. Unexpected random visual targets controlled by a computer were positioned where they could only be seen from above the operating table. During the post-operation recovery phase patients who had undergone the implantation guessed what image was being displayed. No significant results beyond the limits of chance were found.
- **Blackmore (1991)** found that 12% of people reported having OBEs and noted a similar figure of 8% from an Icelandic study. However, a rate of 50% was found among heavy marijuana users.

Evaluation

- Blackmore (1982) believes that OBEs occur if a person loses contact with sensory inputs, while perceptions occur from elsewhere, while still awake, suggesting the phenomenon is a dream state experience.
- There is evidence for OBEs from different sources, backing up the idea of separate subtypes, e.g. Poynton (1975) finds similar patterns of occurrences to Green (1968), with research from different countries.
- One possible practical application of research into OBEs is the creation of video games that give a sense of high levels of reality. It may also be possible for surgeons to operate on people great distances away, by controlling a robotic, virtual self.
- Ehrsson et al.'s (2007) research (see above) suggests that OBEs occur due to a disruption of our usual perception of having a self located behind our eyes, replacing this with a new viewpoint from elsewhere. Blackmore (2007) praises this particular research for bringing OBEs into the laboratory, allowing theories of how such phenomena occur to be tested under controlled, scientific conditions.
- Moody (1998) reports, after years of studying NDEs, that they are wonderful experiences, typically consisting of a buzzing noise, a sense of blissful peace, moving into light and meeting people associated with religion. However, this

seems to be a very selective view of NDEs, as 15% of people experiencing them describe them as 'hellish' and frightening, suggesting that research in this area may often be invalid due to researcher bias and poor methodology.

- The fact that the sensation of 'entering a tunnel' is a common occurrence with both OBEs and NDEs has been interpreted by some as a religious experience. However, as it is always a tunnel and not a door or similar, and tunnel-like experiences also occur with epilepsy, falling asleep, meditation and some drug use, this suggests that the experience may be understood by reference to brain structures.
- Blackmore (1991) believes that NDEs provide no evidence for life after death, and are best understood by reference to neurochemistry, physiology and psychology.

Psychic mediumship

Psychic mediumship involves having special powers that allow communication of messages from the afterlife. Mediums fulfil the role of helping people come to terms with the death of loved ones. There are two general subtypes.

- **Physical mediums** — physical phenomena are demonstrated at séances that are viewable by those sitting with the medium. Spirit people communicate to the living by raps, audible figures and materialised figures.
- **Mental mediums** — mental phenomena are demonstrated through the mind of a medium. This can occur in four ways:
  - **clairvoyance** (where a medium sees a spirit)
  - **clairaudience** (where a medium hears a spirit)
  - **clairsentience** (where a medium senses the presence and thoughts of a spirit)
  - **trance mediumship** (where a medium is overshadowed by a spirit communicator speaking directly through the medium)

> **Research**

- **Beischel and Schwarz (2007)** tested the anomalous reception of material about deceased persons received by mediums under rigorous experimental conditions that eliminated other explanations. Eight established mediums were used with eight student participant 'sitters', four of whom had lost a parent and four who had lost a peer. Each deceased parent was paired with a same-gender deceased peer. Sitters were not present at readings, with an experimenter who was blind to information about the sitters and the deceased acting as a proxy sitter. The mediums, blind to the identities of the sitters and the deceased, each read two absent sitters and their paired deceased. Each pair of sitters was read by two mediums. Each blinded sitter then read two itemised transcripts, one intended for themselves and the other for the paired control reading and had to choose the reading more applicable to them. Significantly higher findings were obtained for intended versus control readings, suggesting that some mediums can anomalously receive information about deceased people.
- **Rock et al. (2008)** asked eight psychic mediums to describe, independently, their experience of receiving information from a **discarnate** (a deceased loved one). Seven common themes were found:
  - multi-modal sensory impressions concerning the discarnate
  - visual images of the discarnate in the medium's 'mind's eye'

> **Knowledge check 24**
> Explain what is meant by near-death and out-of-body-experiences.

psychic mediumship a claimed ability to experience contact with the spirit world

- 'hearing' information from the discarnate in the medium's 'mind's ear'
- 'feeling' the discarnate's illness/cause of death
- experiencing aromas associated with the discarnate
- empathy with the discarnate
- alteration of mood while in contact with the discarnate
- **Rock and Beischel (2008)** gave seven mediums counterbalanced sequences of a discarnate reading and a control condition. The discarnate reading consisted of a phone reading, including questions about a discarnate where only a blinded reader and a blinded experimenter were on the phone. The control condition consisted of a phone conversation between the medium and the experimenter in which the medium was asked similar questions about a living person known to the medium. Significant differences were found between the discarnate and control readings in regard to how the person being read was experienced, with an altered state of consciousness apparent during discarnate readings, suggesting that a medium is a conduit enabling a discarnate to communicate to a loved one.
- **Schwartz et al. (2001)** asked five mediums to interview a woman who had experienced six significant losses in the last decade. The woman answered only yes or no to questions to cut down on the chances of the mediums' using intuitive reasoning. The mediums performed at an accuracy level of 83%, compared with 36% for control interviewers, suggesting a real psychic effect.

Examiner tip

When answering questions on psychic mediumship, focus could be on several things (as with other examples of exceptional experience): (i) the different ways in which psychic mediumship could occur; (ii) why individuals would feel the need to believe in psychic mediumship; (iii) whether research supports its existence, and also criticism of methodologies used to investigate the phenomenon.

Evaluation

- Lester (2005) concludes from a review of studies and the research methods employed that historical mediumship research lacks the proper research design, statistical power and elimination of proper sources of error necessary to be valid studies of the phenomena.
- Laboratory-based research into the authenticity of psychic mediumship needs to strike a balance between optimising the mediumship process for both the medium and the assumed spirit in order to increase the probability of capturing the phenomenon if it exists, as well as creating research methods maximising the experimental 'blinding' of the medium, the rater and the experimenter in order to eliminate other explanations. If this balance is achieved, it will optimise the chances of getting positive results while establishing rigorous controlled conditions.
- The evidence from research into psychic mediumship produces results similar to other areas of paranormal experiences, in that positive results are gained with believers but not with unbelievers, suggesting that results cannot be accepted until replicated by independent observers.
- There may be a biased tendency to focus on events/facts from mediums that are true, and to ignore those that are not.
- Research into psychic mediumship especially raises ethical concerns, as those involved may often be grieving for loved ones. Procedures should therefore be applied to eliminate any possibility of harm.

- Kelly (2008) believes that most mediums are not intentional frauds, but exploit vulnerable people emotionally. She believes that psychic mediumship is merely empathetic intuition or 'cold reading', where mediums tell people seemingly amazing facts they could only know by psychic methods, but which actually just misuse statistical probability to make them seem plausible.

Knowledge check 25

In what ways is it claimed that psychic mediumship can occur?

Summary

- Pseudoscience is a body of supposedly scientific knowledge that fails to comply with scientific methods.
- The scientific status of parapsychology revolves around the legitimacy of studying paranormal phenomena, the research methods employed and the refusal of sceptics to contemplate their existence.
- The Ganzfeld technique tests for ESP, with believers claiming significant results, but sceptics reporting methodological failings.
- Psychokinesis sees the mind affecting matter by invisible means, with independent researchers often unable to replicate significant findings.
- Coincidences and errors in probability judgements lead to paranormal claims, with several cognitive factors affecting the ability to calculate probability and create assumptions that coincidental events are planned.
- Superstitious behaviour involves a need for control and certainty and is explicable through operant conditioning, while magical thinking sees all things as connected by paranormal forces based on symbolism and the laws of similarity and contagion.
- Personality factors underlying anomalous experience include neuroticism and defensiveness, with extroversion associated with ESP abilities, and an additional role for locus of control linked to a belief in fate and control through willpower.
- Research into psychic healing suggests a biological explanation; there is a link to sleep and dream states for OBEs and NDEs, while psychic mediumship arouses arguments over its authenticity, though it does have a role in helping people come to term with the death of loved ones.

Psychological research and scientific method

Application of scientific method in psychology

Major features of science

Science is a system of acquiring knowledge and is defined as the observation, identification, description, experimental investigation (scientific method), and theoretical explanation of phenomena.

The scientific method has four parts:

- observation and description of a phenomenon or group of phenomena
- formulation of a hypothesis to explain the phenomena

scientific method
a means of acquiring knowledge based on observable, measureable evidence

- use of the hypothesis to predict the existence of other phenomena, or to predict quantitatively the results of new observations
- performance of experimental tests of the predictions by several independent experimenters and properly performed experiments

The most important feature of science is its dependence on **empirical methods** of observation and investigation. This involves observations based upon sensory experiences (via the senses) rather than simply upon thoughts and beliefs. Therefore, a scientific idea is one that has been subjected to empirical testing by the use of rigorous observations of events and/or phenomena. For science to make sense there must be an explanation of empirically observed phenomena and this is achieved by developing theories that can be tested and improved by empiricism.

Science therefore involves making predictions and testing them by scientific observations (empirical ones). Such observations are made without bias or expectation by the researcher and are performed under controlled conditions. In this way theories and hypotheses are validated (found to be true) or falsified (found to be untrue). It is the belief that this ability to predict and control behaviour under experimental conditions can also be achieved in real-life settings which makes the study of psychology opt for scientific investigation as its selected path towards the acquisition of knowledge.

- **Replicability** — confidence in psychological findings is increased by replication of investigations as part of the validation process. This involves repeating research under the same conditions. It is important that scientific research is written up fully and clearly to allow it to be properly replicated, thus establishing its reliability and validity. Fleischmann and Pons (1989) claimed to have created cold fusion (a form of low-energy nuclear reaction) in the laboratory, raising hopes of abundant and cheap sources of energy. However, enthusiasm waned when replications of their experimental technique failed to produce the same results. They had either witnessed a separate phenomenon or had made errors in their procedures. Only by replication were scientists able to arrive at this conclusion.
- Objectivity — an important feature of scientific research is that it should be objective, that is to say perceived without distortion by personal feelings or interpretation. Objectivity is therefore an integral part of empiricism, where observations made derive from sensory experience and not from the biased viewpoint of the researcher. Such bias is often unconscious with no deliberate attempt by the researcher to produce certain results. For example, results from Ganzfeld studies, which test for the existence of ESP (see above, under anomalistic psychology) tend to match the beliefs of the researcher. Therefore, those researchers who believe or feel that ESP may be real tend to find results supporting such a belief, while those who are sceptical about these claims tend to find results refuting the existence of ESP. Cyril Burt was a psychologist famous for his work on the inheritance of intelligence. However, his research on IQ and twins was found to be deliberately false and this probably occurred because Burt's biased, subjective views about the inheritance of intelligence led to lack of objectivity. It was due to this lack of objectivity that false findings were accepted as true, leading to flawed practical applications.
- Falsification — part of the verification (validation) process is the idea of falsification, where replication of its exact research procedures is the accepted

empiricism the belief that sensory experience is the only source of knowledge

Examiner tip

When answering questions on the application of scientific method in psychology, draw upon your knowledge of this area from your AS studies, as the specification at A2 builds on what you learned there, for example, what is meant by replication? However, to access the higher levels of marks, a deeper understanding, accessible through what you study at A2, will be necessary.

replication repetition of research to authenticate results

objectivity observations that are made without bias

Examiner tip

When explaining features such as objectivity, try to include relevant examples in order to create detail and show understanding, for instance, that results from Ganzfeld studies, which search for evidence of extrasensory perception abilities, are affected by whether researchers believe in, or are sceptical of, ESP.

falsification that scientific statements are capable of being proven wrong

manner of determining whether a scientific theory or hypothesis is false. The psychodynamic approach in psychology, associated with the work of Freud, is often criticised for being unfalsifiable. Freud's account of personality allowed him to place interpretations on behaviour that could not be shown to be untrue. For example Freud might argue that someone behaves in a certain fashion due to events in their infancy and if the person agrees this to be so then it is seen as supporting Freud. However, if the person disagrees, it is still seen as supporting Freud, as he would argue that they are in fact repressing experiences from their infancy.

Scientific investigation

The chosen method of scientific investigation is the **laboratory-based experiment**. This method permits a great deal of control over extraneous variables. Any change in the dependent variable (DV) is perceived as being due to manipulation of the independent variable (IV) and in this way **causality** (cause-and-effect relationships) can be established.

There are other methods of hypothesis testing, but they have reduced ability to determine causality. Such methods include **field** and **natural** experiments, but even non-experimental methods can be performed using the scientific method, such as naturalistic observations. Objectivity can also be attempted by using methods like **inter-observer reliability**, where researchers make efforts to ensure that they observe phenomena and events in identical, unbiased ways. Results can therefore be claimed as valid.

Psychology is often seen as a 'soft science' (unlike physics and chemistry, which are hard sciences) because it tries to use deterministic and reductionist principles of science but due to the subjective subject matter research cannot be carried out with the usual rigor.

Validating new knowledge and the role of peer review

Part of the scientific verification process, where research is deemed to be acceptable or unacceptable in scientific terms, is the peer-review system. This system is considered fundamental to scientific and scholarly communication and is used by scientists to determine whether research findings should be published in a scientific journal. The peer-review system subjects scientific research papers to independent scrutiny by scientific experts in that field (peers) before a decision is made about whether they can be made public. So important is the peer-review system that it is often referred to as 'the arbiter of scientific quality' and is perceived as a security or filter system designed to reduce the chances of flawed or unscientific research being accepted as fact. The peer-review system operates on the basis of belief that the status of research results is as important as the findings themselves.

Science is increasingly important in all walks of life, not just psychology, and scientific developments are often the subject of news headlines and public interest. There is an increasing amount of scientific information being made public, as well as a growing number of bodies and organisations promoting and discussing scientific research, like drug companies in the medical world, and therefore it is often difficult to decide

Knowledge check 26

Summarise the main features of science.

peer review the scrutiny of research papers by experts to determine their scientific validity

Examiner tip

Be sure when studying the peer review process that you can construct all the types of answer required. You could be asked to explain briefly what is meant by peer review, outline how the process occurs or detail the weaknesses of the system. You could even be asked to outline and evaluate the process as a mini-essay.

which research is worthy of consideration and which is spurious, especially when different scientists are arguing from completely different viewpoints.

Over 1 million research papers are published in scientific journals each year, but although the peer-review system is recognised and used by scientists all over the world as the best means of assessing scientific plausibility, the general public knows little, if anything, about this verification process. However, it is important that the public (especially those people who deal with scientific claims, e.g. patient groups) are aware of the concept and ask whether research has passed public scrutiny before it is accepted as true, in order to avoid the frustration and damage that comes from the acceptance of poor scientific research.

The peer-review process

During the peer-review process it is normal for two or three expert reviewers to be sent copies of a researcher's work by a journal editor. These reviewers report back to the editor, highlighting any weaknesses or problem areas and making suggestions for improvement if necessary. There are generally four options for the reviewers to recommend:

- Accept the work unconditionally.
- Accept it as long as the researcher improves it in certain ways.
- Reject it, but suggest revisions and a resubmission.
- Reject it outright.

Criticisms of peer review

Critics argue that peer review is not as unbiased as it claims to be. Research is carried out in a narrow social world and social relationships within that world affect objectivity and impartiality. In obscure research areas it may not be possible to find people of sufficient knowledge levels to carry out a proper peer review. There have even been accusations that some scientists' ability to consider research in an unbiased and professional manner is compromised by the fact that they are being funded by organisations with a vested interest in certain research being deemed scientifically acceptable. One way of attempting to address this is to ensure that reviewers are anonymous and independent.

The peer-review process is a slow one, sometimes taking months or even years to complete. A further criticism is that peer review creates controlling elites with the power to publish or not which are vulnerable to personal jealousies. There may be resistance to revolutionary ideas that go against the elite or prevailing views, supporting Kuhn's idea that science does not advance steadily, but through one paradigm being toppled and replaced with another.

Knowledge check 27

Peer review is supposed to be the 'arbiter of scientific quality', subjecting research findings to unbiased, independent scrutiny so that flawed research is not accepted as true. However, what criticisms can be made of the system?

The consequences of false or unscientific research being accepted as true can be serious, not least because many other scientists' subsequent research may be built upon the fact of the original research being accepted as true. Cyril Burt, who was found to have falsified research into the heritability of intelligence, was a major figure in the field and his research findings, widely accepted by the psychological community as true, greatly influenced the approach of subsequent researchers who often took his work as a starting point for their own research.

Designing psychological investigations

Selection and application of appropriate research methods

There are various **research methods**, each with advantages and disadvantages and each of which suits different research situations and aims.

- **Experiments** — regarded as the most scientific form of research and are the only method establishing **causality** (cause-and-effect relationships). Although operating in somewhat artificial conditions, they are probably the best method where circumstances permit their use. The laboratory experiment is the most preferred type as it allows strict control over variables and conditions. Field and natural experiments occur in more natural circumstances but with reduced control over variables and conditions. Field experiments use artificially induced independent variables, whereas natural experiments use naturally occurring ones.
- **Correlations** — performed when relationships are being investigated (i.e. when looking at the degree of similarity between two co-variables). They show direction and intensity of relationships, but cannot establish causality or investigate non-linear associations. Correlations can sometimes be used when experiments would be ethically unsuitable. They can also be used to identify areas of interest worthy of further experimental investigation.
- **Self-reports** — questionnaires, interviews and surveys are used to gain information directly from participants about themselves. Lots of data can generally be gained in a relatively short period of time, though causality cannot be established and there are risks of idealised and socially desirable answers. Interviews, unlike questionnaires and surveys, require a face-to-face interaction with the interviewer. They can be used to identify areas worthy of further research by more stringent means.
- **Observations** — conducted where the emphasis is on studying natural behaviour in a natural environment (although observations can also be conducted under laboratory conditions). Causality cannot be established and replication is often difficult, but ecological validity is high.
- **Longitudinal studies** — conducted over a long time period, usually at set intervals, where trends (changes over time) need to be considered. Causality cannot be established and **atypical sample attrition** occurs, where participants of a certain type drop out, biasing the sample.
- **Case studies** — conducted on one person or a small group, often to assess their unique circumstances or to find the source of a problem. They provide rich and detailed data that can be used to form effective individual treatments, but their findings cannot be generalised to others, nor can they establish causality.

research methods experimental and non-experimental means of conducting practical investigations

Implications of sampling strategies

A sample is a part of a target population used for research purposes. The general idea is that what is true for a sample will be true for the population from which the sample is drawn and which it represents. There are several **sampling** methods used in psychology and these entail implications for bias and generalising.

sampling the selection of part of a target population for research purposes

Examiner tip

If answering a question involving random sampling, do not fall into the trap of thinking it guarantees a representative sample and presenting this as a strength of the sampling method. Random sampling does not guarantee this, as it is quite possible for unbiased selection to produce a totally unrepresentative sample, for instance all male or all female.

Knowledge check 28

(a) Why might random sampling not produce a representative sample?
(b) What types of sample produce more representative samples?

reliability measures of consistency within sets of scores and over time

- **Random sampling** — a random sample occurs where any members of a target population are selected without bias, to any of the testing conditions. This can be achieved for instance by drawing names out of a hat, or the use of random number tables. A truly random sample is, however, difficult to obtain, as generally all members of a target population will not be available for selection. Also a random sample is not necessarily representative because random selection could theoretically provide a biased sample (e.g. all females), making generalisation difficult.
- **Opportunity sampling** — opportunity samples are popular. They are generally easier to obtain because use is made of people's availability. These types of sample are often biased (those available may be a certain unrepresentative type of person, e.g. all shoppers) and are therefore difficult to generalise from.
- **Self-selected (volunteer) sampling** — volunteer samples are generally recruited using advertisements or posters and therefore require little effort to obtain. However, volunteers tend to be a certain personality type and are therefore unrepresentative. They are often keen to help and therefore more at risk of demand characteristics.
- **Systematic sampling** — systematic samples are obtained by selecting every nth person (e.g. every fifth one). This is an unbiased method of selection, producing fairly representative samples.
- **Stratified sampling** — stratified samples select groups of participants in proportion to their frequency in the target population. Individuals for each group (strata) are randomly selected to produce a highly representative sample. If random sampling is not used for the strata this is known as **quota sampling.**

Issues of reliability

The term reliability is used to describe consistency. **Internal reliability** concerns the extent to which there is consistency within a process, for example that all the components of a psychological test are measuring the same thing. **External reliability** concerns the extent to which a measure of something is consistent with other measures of the same thing.

If findings from research are replicated consistently, they are said to be reliable. There are several ways in which reliability can be assessed and improved.
- **Inter-observer (rater) reliability** — concerns the extent to which there is agreement between different observers involved in observing behaviour. For instance if two observers agree on the type of play children are involved in then they have inter-observer reliability, but if one observer categorises a child as involved in cooperative play while another observer categorises it as rough and tumble play then they do not have inter-observer reliability. Observers should ideally have agreed operational definitions of the key categories being observed.
- **Split-half method** — a means of assessing the extent to which individual items in a test or questionnaire are consistent with each other. The method involves splitting the test or questionnaire into two halves after the data have been obtained (e.g. comparing results from the odd questions with the even questions). If the results from the two halves have high correlation, they are reliable; if not, the test needs revising.

- **Kuder–Richardson method** — concerns all the possible ways in which a test can be split in half and is therefore a very rigorous method of assessing reliability.
- **Test re-test** — measures the stability of a test or interview etc. over time. It involves giving the same test to the same participants on two occasions. If the same result is obtained, reliability is established.

Reliability is an important concept in itself but is also important in that validity cannot be established without reliability being established first, although reliability does not guarantee validity.

Assessing and improving validity

The term validity describes accuracy, the degree to which something is measuring what it claims to measure. Validity therefore refers to the legitimacy of studies and the extent to which findings can be generalised beyond the research setting as a consequence of a study's **internal** and **external** validity.

- **Internal validity** — concerns the extent to which the observed effect is attributable to the experimental manipulation (the influence of the IV on the DV) and not some other factor, in other words the test is measuring what it claims to measure. It could be argued Milgram's electric shock study was internally valid, as participants believed it to be real.
- **External validity** — concerns the extent to which an experimental effect can be generalised to other settings (**ecological validity**), other people (**population validity**) and over time (**historical validity**). It could be argued that Milgram's electric shock study lacked external validity as it is not a usual occurrence to shock people for getting questions wrong, it only used male participants and was a product of its time.
- **Face (content) validity** — a simple way of assessing validity involving the extent to which items look like what the test claims to measure.
- **Concurrent validity** — assesses validity by correlating scores on a test with those from another test known to be valid.
- **Predictive validity** — similar to concurrent validity but the two sets of scores are obtained at differing points in time, showing for instance that a test allows accurate predictions of future behaviour.

Ethical considerations in the design and conduct of psychological research

When designing and conducting research care should be taken to address all possible ethical considerations so that participants are protected from harm and their dignity remains intact.

Psychology needs to conduct research so that theories can be generated and tested, allowing the subject to develop and possibly produce practical applications beneficial to society founded on solid scientific practices and principles. If such research is conducted in an unethical manner, then the subject will not have a high and respectable public profile and people will be reluctant to participate in future research, meaning that the subject cannot advance or be of positive use. It is true

Examiner tip
Questions on reliability and validity at A2 are likely to expect a deeper understanding of the concepts than was required at AS. As well as being able to explain the terms, an understanding of different types of reliability and validity will be needed, and knowledge of how to assess and improve them.

validity the degree to which results can be generalised beyond the research setting

ethical considerations measures taken to protect participants from harm and to retain their dignity

Examiner tip

You may be asked about ethical issues that arise in psychological research, but could also be asked about strategies to deal with ethical issues. Make sure you read questions carefully and give the answer required. Questions could also focus specifically on ethical issues to consider when designing or carrying out investigations.

that, in the past, unethical research has taken place, giving the study of psychology a negative profile. Ethical guidelines are in place to try to stop this situation recurring.

- **Informed consent** — participants are given all details of the intended research so that they can make a considered decision as to whether to participate. To perform research on people below the age of 16 and those incapable of giving informed consent, like the mentally disordered, informed consent must be gained from parents or legal guardians. In research where deceit is inevitable (to conceal hypotheses) it may be possible to debrief participants fully after the research, giving them an opportunity to withdraw their data at that point.
- **Presumptive consent** — a means of getting informed consent from non-participants without revealing the hypotheses to the real participants. People similar to those who will participate are given full details and asked if they would participate. If they agree, then it can be presumed that it is acceptable to perform the research.
- **Prior general consent** — performs the same function as presumptive consent, but participants agree to not be informed (i.e. they agree to be deceived, but without knowing how or when).
- **Right to withdraw** — participants are given the right to withdraw from an investigation at any point, including the withdrawal of their data after research has occurred. No attempts should be made to persuade people to continue when they do not want to do so.
- **Deceit** — participants should not be deceived. Informed consent is not possible where any instances of deceit occur.
- **Protection from harm** — participants should leave an experiment in the same physical and psychological state in which they entered it. They should not incur any physical or psychological harm by participating. No research procedure or practice should subject participants to levels of risk outside those they would normally encounter. There is a debate within psychology as to whether this principle extends to animals. Giving participants a full debriefing after research has occurred helps to reduce the risk of harm. If any unexpected harm does occur it is the responsibility of the investigator to attend to it (e.g. by the provision of counselling).
- **Debriefing** — not an ethical issue in itself but is a way of dealing with issues like harm and informed consent. Participants are told all details of the research and are reassured about their performance. The right to withdraw should again be emphasised.
- **Inducement to take part** — participants should not receive any form of inducement (e.g. payment) to take part in research. The ability to consider rationally whether to give informed consent is compromised by inducements to participate.
- **Confidentiality/anonymity** — two related ethical considerations. Details of participants' identities and performances in research should not be made public. Participants must consent to any uses to which research findings will be put before research commences.
- **Ethical committees** — comprising experts in the field and concerned bodies who consider all facets of potential research and come to a decision as to whether research is ethical and can proceed.

- **Cost–benefit analysis** — a means of comparing potential costs against possible benefits to decide whether research should proceed. If benefits exceed costs, then a decision to proceed can be taken.
- **Observations** — should only be conducted in circumstances where people would normally expect to be observed.

Knowledge check 29

Why were ethical guidelines introduced into psychology?

Data analysis and reporting on investigations

Appropriate selection of graphical representations

Graphical representations display data in pictorial fashion, permitting an easily understandable alternative to numerical presentations. There are several types of graph, each used in different circumstances. Graphs should be titled and each axis, horizontal (x) and vertical (y) should be labelled. The vertical axis usually represents the DV (frequency).

graphical representations easily understood pictorial representations of data

Bar chart

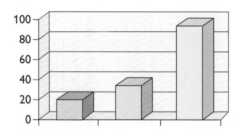

Figure 1 Bar graph of means for nominal IV

The height of the bar represents frequency and bar charts differ from histograms as empty categories can be excluded (see Figure 1). There is no true zero and data on the horizontal axis are not continuous.

Histogram

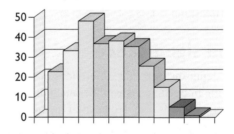

Figure 2 Frequency histogram for interval IV

A histogram (see Figure 2) is very similar to a bar chart but the area within the bars is proportional to the frequencies represented, the horizontal axis is continuous and there are no gaps between the bars.

Frequency polygon

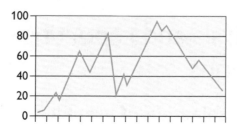

Figure 3 Frequency polygon for interval IV

This type of graph is an alternative to the histogram and is used when two or more frequency distributions need to be compared on the same graph. The frequency polygon (see Figure 3) is drawn by linking the midpoints from the top of each bar in a histogram.

Scattergram

Examiner tip
You will not have to construct graphs but you must be able to select graphs for different circumstances and describe their features, as well as having knowledge of suitable examples. All graphs should have a title identifying the type of graph and what is being represented. The horizontal (x) and the vertical (y) axes should be labelled, with units of measurement identified.

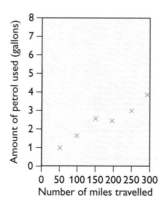

Figure 4a Positive correlation

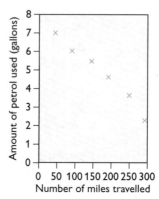

Figure 4b Negative correlation

This type of graph allows representation of the degree of correlation (similarity) between two co-variables. Scattergrams can display both positive (Figure 4a) and negative (Figure 4b) correlations.

Probability and significance

Psychological research generally looks for differences or relationships between sets of data. However, of prime importance is whether such differences and relationships are *significant* ones, in other words they are beyond the boundaries of chance.

If a coin is tossed 100 times, by the law of averages the result would be 50 heads and 50 tails. However, a possible result is 52 heads and 48 tails. There is therefore a difference between the two sets of data, but is that difference beyond the boundaries of chance? Probably not in this case, but how would we determine the cut-off point between the two sets of data being significant or insignificant? 55 heads to 45 tails? 60 to 40? This is where the idea of probability comes in.

Probability concerns the degree of certainty that an observed difference or relationship between two sets of data is a real difference/relationship, or has occurred by chance factors. It is never 100% certain that such differences and relationships are real ones (i.e. beyond the boundaries of chance), which is why it is impossible to prove something beyond all doubt. An accepted cut-off point is needed therefore and in psychology, and in science generally, a significance level (probability level) of $p \leq$ 0.05 is used. This means that there is a 5% possibility an observed difference or relationship between two sets of data is actually not a real difference one but has occurred by chance factors. This is deemed to be an acceptable level of error.

On certain occasions a stricter, more stringent level of significance may be needed (e.g. if testing out new, untried drugs or in new research areas). Then a significance level of $p \leq 0.01$ might be used, meaning that we can be 99% certain that an observed difference/relationship is a real one, but that there is still a 1% chance it has occurred because of chance factors. If an even stricter level of $p \leq 0.001$ was used, this would mean we are 99.9% sure it is a real difference/relationship, but that there is still a 0.1% chance that it occurred by chance.

Type 1 and type 2 errors

A type 1 error occurs when a difference/relationship is accepted as a real one (i.e. beyond the boundaries of chance) but this is wrong because the significance level has been set too high. This means that the null hypothesis would be wrongly rejected. With a 5% significance level this means, on average, for every 100 significant differences/relationships found, 5 of them will have been wrongly accepted.

A type 2 error occurs when a difference/relationship is accepted as being insignificant (i.e. not a real difference/relationship) and this is wrong because the significance level has been set too low (e.g. 1%). This means that the null hypothesis would be wrongly rejected.

A 5% significance level is the accepted level, as it strikes a balance between making type 1 and type 2 errors.

Factors affecting choice of statistical test

When research is performed, data are produced and, having set a significance level of 5%, an appropriate statistical test will need to be chosen to analyse the data to see whether they are significant or not (beyond the boundaries of chance). Four statistical tests are referred to in the specification (though many others exist) and there are various criteria that can be used to determine which one to use.

Levels of data measurement

Decide first which of the following data levels applies.
- **Nominal** — the data occur as frequencies/categories (e.g. how many people prefer Pepsi or Coke).
- **Ordinal** — the data occur as ranks (e.g. the finishing places, 1st, 2nd, 3rd etc. in a running race).

probability the likelihood of events being determined by chance

significance level a statistical criterion to determine if observed differences/relationships are beyond the boundaries of chance

Knowledge check 30

Explain what is meant by the concepts of probability and significance in psychology.

statistical test mathematical means of analysing data

- **Ratio** — the data occur as units of equal size, but with a true zero point (e.g. inches on a ruler).
- **Interval** — the data occur as units of equal size, but using both positive and negative numbers.

Test of difference or of correlation

It needs to be determined if research is looking for a difference or a relationship between two sets of data. If a relationship is being looked for, a **Spearman's rho** test is used. If a difference is being sought, a **Wilcoxon matched-pairs, signed-ranks** test, a **Mann–Whitney** test or a **Chi-squared** test is used.

Experimental design

If samples are related, that is to say, all participants do all conditions of an experiment, then a repeated measures design will have been used and therefore a Wilcoxon test needs to be performed. (As a matched-pairs design is a special kind of repeated measures design, its use should also lead to performing the Wilcoxon test.) If the data are at least ordinal and samples are independent (i.e. participants only do one condition of an experiment), a Mann–Whitney test should be used. If the data are nominal (occur as frequencies) and samples independent, select the Chi-squared test.

Knowledge check 31

What three factors need to be considered when selecting a statistical test?

Use of inferential analysis

Inferential tests are those showing how likely it is that patterns observed in sets of data occur by chance and whether it is possible to infer (deduce) that the same patterns exist in the general population. The specification requires knowledge of four main tests.

- **Chi-squared test** — used when a difference is predicted to occur between two sets of data, the data are of at least nominal level (occur as frequencies) and an independent measures design has been used (participants only perform one condition of an experiment). It is also possible to use Chi-squared as a test of association (relationship).
- **Mann–Whitney test** — used when a difference is predicted to occur between two sets of data, the data are of at least ordinal level (occur as ranks) and an independent groups design has been used.
- **Wilcoxon matched-pairs, signed-ranks** — used when a difference is predicted to occur between two sets of data, the data are of at least ordinal level (occur as ranks) and a repeated or matched pairs design has been used.
- **Spearman's rho test** — used when a relationship (correlation) is predicted to occur between two sets of data, the data are of at least ordinal level (occur as ranks) and the data are pairs of scores from the same person or event.

Examiner tip
You will not be required to carry out statistical tests but must have a working knowledge of them in order that the correct test could be selected from information given. To achieve this it is essential to have knowledge of factors affecting the choice of test, including levels of measurement.

Statistical analysis produces an **observed** value, which is compared with a **critical** value in order to determine if the observed value is significant (beyond the boundaries of chance). Critical value tables need to be referenced, taking into consideration information such as whether a hypothesis is directional or non-directional (one-tailed or two-tailed), the number of participants or participant pairs (N) used and what level of significance (e.g. 5%) is being used. The Mann–Whitney and Wilcoxon tests require observed values to be equal to or less than the critical value to be accepted as significant, allowing the null hypothesis to be rejected. The Chi-squared and Spearman's rho tests require an observed value to be equal to or greater than the critical value to be accepted as significant, allowing the null hypothesis to be rejected.

Analysis and interpretation of qualitative data

Qualitative data are non-numerical, for instance a narrative of what was said in an interview, or a child's drawing. Such data provide insight into feelings and thoughts that quantitative data cannot reveal. When analysing such data, researchers generally look for underlying meanings and this can be a subjective task based on the researchers' own interpretations. There are ways, however, of converting qualitative data into quantitative data so that they can be more objectively analysed by statistical means. This generally involves converting the data into categories or themes. An example is **content analysis**, which involves counting the frequencies of occurrences (e.g. the number of presents and their sizes could be counted in children's drawings of a Christmas tree and presents).

qualitative data
information that occurs in a non-numerical form

Conventions of reporting on psychological investigations

When research studies have been conducted, they may be published as research papers in respected academic journals after having been peer-reviewed. There is a conventional, accepted way of presenting such research in set sections.

research papers
investigation reports that are written to a conventional format

(1) The **abstract** gives a summary of the research, entailing key details of aim(s), hypotheses, participants, methods and procedures, findings and conclusions.

(2) The **introduction** presents a review of associated and related previous research studies and theories. This should have a logical progression into the aims and hypotheses.

(3) The **method** section presents details of the type of method used, independent and dependent variables (or co-variables in the case of a correlation), controls, sampling details, ethical considerations, procedures etc., in short, all details necessary to permit an exact replication. Any tests and questionnaires used should be placed in the appendices, but be referred to here.

(4) The **results** section presents a description of the results, comprising a summary of the raw data and measures of central tendency and dispersion in written form, as well as in appropriate graphs and tables. Details of inferential statistical analyses are also included, indicating whether results are significant or not. Actual raw data and statistical calculations, although referred to, are not included here and should be placed in the appendices.

(5) The **discussion** section assesses the findings in terms of previous research studies and theories, and outlines limitations of the research and suggests possible modifications to deal with these. This section also proposes ideas for future research and outlines the implications of such research.

(6) The **appendices** include all raw data, questionnaires, calculations, references, material used etc.

Examiner tip
Although you are not assessed in your ability to carry out practical investigations, it is advised that research is carried out, because questions could be asked about how and why such studies are written up in a set way. The best way to achieve this is to have written up some research of your own.

Knowledge check 32
Why do practical investigations have to be written in a conventional manner?

Summary

- Science is a system of acquiring knowledge, based upon replicability, objectivity, theory construction, hypothesis testing and the use of empirical methods.

- New knowledge is authenticated through peer review, which assesses scientific validity of research before publication. However, critics claim it is not an unbiased or flawless process.

- The designing of scientific investigations involves the selection and application of appropriate research methods, as well as the consideration of implications of sampling strategies, issues of reliability and validity and ethical concerns.

- Data analysis and reporting of psychological investigations involves appropriate selection of graphs, as well as consideration of probability and significance levels, factors affecting choice of statistical tests, the use of inferential analysis and the conventions of reporting on scientific investigations.

AQA(A) A2 Psychology

The examination

The Unit 4 examination lasts 2 hours and has three sections: A, B and C. In section A (Psychopathology) there will be three essay-style questions from which you must answer one. In section B (Psychology in Action) there will be three essay-style questions from which you must answer one. In section C (Psychological Research and Scientific Method) there will be one compulsory structured question.

Each question in section A and B is worth 24 marks overall, although some questions may be split into parts. The compulsory question in section C is worth 35 marks.

To guarantee being able to answer a question in section A, you must ensure you have studied and revised all the subject content listed in the specification for either schizophrenia, depression or anxiety disorders. To guarantee being able to answer a question in section B, you must ensure you have studied and revised all the subject content listed in the specification for either media psychology, the psychology of addictive behaviour or anomalistic psychology. To guarantee being able to answer the compulsory structured question in section C, you must ensure you have studied and revised all the subject content listed in the specification for psychological research and scientific method.

This paper will account for 50% of the total A2 marks and 25% of the total A-level (AS + A2).

Assessment objectives

In this psychology examination, three sets of skills or 'assessment objectives' are tested: AO1, AO2 and AO3.

Assessment objective 1 (AO1)

This concerns questions designed to test your knowledge and understanding of psychological theories, terminology, concepts, studies and methods. You should be able to:
- recognise, recall and show understanding of knowledge
- select, organise and communicate relevant information in a variety of forms
- present and organise material clearly
- use relevant psychological terminology

Assessment objective 2 (AO2)

This concerns questions designed to test your knowledge and understanding of the application of knowledge via analysis and evaluation of psychological theories, concepts, studies and methods. You should be able to:

- analyse and evaluate knowledge and processes
- apply knowledge and processes to novel situations, including those relating to issues
- assess the validity, reliability and credibility of information

Assessment objective 3 (AO3)

This concerns questions designed to test your knowledge and application of knowledge and understanding of how psychology as a science works. You should be able to:

- describe ethical, safe and skilful practical techniques and processes and the appropriate selection of qualitative and quantitative methods
- know how to make, record and communicate reliable and valid observations and measurements with appropriate accuracy and precision, through using primary and secondary sources
- analyse, interpret, explain and evaluate the methodology, results and impact of experimental and investigative activities in a variety of ways

For each question in sections A and B there are 8 AO1 marks, 12 AO2 marks and 4 AO3 marks. For the compulsory structured question in section C there are 3 AO1 marks, 4 AO2 marks and 28 AO3 marks (a total of 83 marks on offer). You may sit this exam in either January or June of each year.

Effective examination performance

For AO1 you should:

- avoid 'story-telling' or 'commonsense' answers that lack psychological content
- give some depth to your answers and not just provide a list of points
- achieve a balance between the breadth and depth of your answer

Make your answer coherent. It should be clearly written and show continuity of thought. It should not read as a series of unconnected comments.

For AO2/AO3 you should:

- elaborate upon evaluative points in order to construct an effective commentary
- where possible and appropriate, make use of both negative and positive criticism, for example methodological faults and practical applications
- draw conclusions and interpretations from your AO1 material
- select material carefully so that it is specifically directed at the question rather than just forming a general answer on the topic area
- avoid overuse of generic evaluation, such as the repetitive detailing of methodological strengths and weaknesses of all the research studies included in your answer
- present arguments and evaluations clearly
- ensure that you have included within your evaluation and analysis evidence of synopticity

Explanation of key examination command words

For AO1

Outline: provide brief details without explanation

Describe: provide a detailed account without explanation

For AO2

Evaluate: assess the value/effectiveness

Discuss: provide a reasoned, balanced account

How the marks are awarded

Mark band descriptors

AO1 mark bands (8 marks)

Marks	Criteria
8 marks	Sound. Knowledge and understanding are accurate and well detailed. A good range of relevant material has been presented. There is substantial evidence of breadth/depth. Organisation and structure of the answer are coherent.
7–5 marks	Reasonable. Knowledge and understanding are generally accurate and reasonably detailed. A range of relevant material has been presented. There is evidence of breadth and/or depth. Organisation and structure of the answer are reasonably coherent.
4–3 marks	Basic. Knowledge and understanding are basic/relatively superficial. A restricted range of material has been presented. Organisation and structure of the answer are basic.
2–1 marks	Rudimentary. Knowledge and understanding are rudimentary and may be muddled and/or inaccurate. The material presented may be brief or largely irrelevant. The answer lacks organisation and structure.
0 marks	No creditworthy material is apparent.

AO2/AO3 mark bands (16 marks)

Marks	Criteria
16–13 marks	Effective. Evaluation shows sound analysis and understanding. Answer is well focused, displaying coherent elaboration and/or a clear line of argument is apparent. Effective use of issues/debates/approaches. There is substantial evidence of synopticity. Well-structured ideas are expressed clearly and fluently. There is consistent, effective use of psychological terminology and appropriate use of grammar, spelling and punctuation.
12–9 marks	Reasonable. Evaluation shows reasonable analysis and evaluation. A generally focused answer, displaying reasonable elaboration and/or a line of argument is apparent. A reasonably effective use of issues/debates/approaches. There is evidence of synopticity. Most ideas are appropriately structured and expressed clearly. There is appropriate use of psychological terminology and some minor errors of grammar; spelling and punctuation only occasionally compromise meaning.

Marks	Criteria
8–5 marks	Basic. Analysis and evaluation demonstrate basic, superficial understanding. The answer is sometimes focused and shows some evidence of elaboration. Superficial reference may be made to issues/debates/approaches. There is some evidence of synopticity. Expression of ideas lacks clarity. Limited use of psychological terminology. Errors of grammar, punctuation and spelling are intrusive.
4–1 marks	Rudimentary. Analysis and evaluation are rudimentary, demonstrating very limited understanding. The answer is weak, muddled and incomplete. Material is not used effectively and may be mainly irrelevant. If reference is made to issues/debates/approaches, it is muddled or inaccurate. There is little or no evidence of synopticity. Deficiency in expression of ideas results in confusion and ambiguity. The answer lacks structure, often merely a series of unconnected assertions. Errors of grammar, punctuation and spelling are frequent and intrusive.
0 marks	No creditworthy material is presented.

Note that each question in sections A and B is awarded a total of 24 marks.

Question 1 **Media psychology (1)**

Outline and evaluate the effects of videos and/or computer games on behaviour.   (24 marks)

ⓔ This is a straightforward essay question taken directly from the specification. Students make a decision whether to offer material on the effects of both videos and computer games on behaviour, or just one of them. If both were offered, less detail would be expected.

Eight marks are available for the outline of the effects of videos and/or computer games, with the remaining 16 marks for the evaluation, with a wealth of research evidence available to use towards this end.

Student answer

Video games **a** permit players an active role and, because they often encourage and glorify violence, the question of influence has centred on whether such behaviour is repeated in real-life scenarios. Funk (1995) **a** found success in video games comes from identifying and selecting violent strategies, supporting **b** the idea that video games do encourage violence. Strasburger and Wilson (2002) **a** found video games desensitise the player to the consequences of violence, creating pro-violence attitudes and suggesting **b** video games have negative consequences, while Cantor (2000) **a** sees video games as demonstrating and reinforcing violence, demonstrating **b** their negative cognitive and behavioural consequences.

Exposure to video games **a** has been argued to retard the development of emotion regulation skills, leading to desensitisation to cues that normally trigger sympathetic responses, with the consequence of an increased likelihood of aggression. Funk (2004) **a** found exposure to video-game violence was indeed **b** linked to lower empathy, while Eron (2001) believes **a** it's emotional desensitisation that blunts empathetic concern and cognitive desensitisation that creates stronger pro-violence attitudes. Overall the evidence from video games research implies **b** that empathy development is retarded, with moral evaluation at a low level, suggesting **b** concern over children's exposure to them.

Although research has identified a relationship between desensitisation and playing video games, desensitisation is difficult to measure **c**, therefore findings may not be valid, plus relationships are correlational **c** and do not display causality.

Other research shows game-playing to have positive aspects for learning and levels of self-esteem **a**. Sanger (1996) found game-playing develops a sense of mastery and control in individuals with low self-esteem, suggesting **b** a positive practical application, while Gee (2003) argues **b** that game-playing offers opportunities for experiential learning, especially in developing social and cultural learning and reasoning skills. Kestanbaum and Weinstein (1985) found **a** game-playing helps adolescent males manage developmental conflicts and safely discharge aggression, suggesting **b** negativity is mainly a parental illusion.

Research has identified important individual, gender and age differences **a**. Dunn and Hughes (2001) found **a** that difficult preschoolers playing video games were

more likely to indulge in aggressive fantasy play, supporting **b** the idea there are individual differences to consider, while Funk and Buchman (1996) found **a** that girls playing video games tended towards greater negative consequences, as their behaviour is seen as violating gender norms, suggesting **b** gender differences do exist. Eisenberg and Fabes (1998) found **a** younger children to be most at risk, because they're still constructing morality, suggesting **b** that the values operating in violent video games will have a greater impact on them than on older individuals with established value systems. One implication **d** of this is that any legal initiatives to restrict or ban the availability of video games should consider their varying impacts on different groupings, though it should be remembered that studies **c** have not focused on the long-term effects of game-playing, plus most studies are of Western cultures **d** and therefore are not representative of other cultures.

There is also evidence that exposure to video games leads to addictive behaviour **a**. Sopes and Millar (1983) found **b** that children playing video games exhibit addictive tendencies, due to the compulsive behavioural involvement, and exhibit withdrawal symptoms, such as shaking, when attempting to stop. There is even some indication of children turning to crime to fund their addiction **a**, demonstrating **b** the social implications of such behaviour.

🅔 An excellent and simply executed essay, of a suitable length within the time constraints. **b** The effects of video games are described in a relevant, accurate and detailed manner, **a** with research studies also used to illustrate pertinent evaluative points. **c** Evaluation additionally centres on relevant methodological points, **d** the implications of restricting or banning video games, as well as the cultural nature of much of the research in this area. The essay has an organised structure to it, permitting the high level of coherence evident in the answer.

(AOI = 8/8) + (AO2/AO3 = 16/16) = 24/24 marks

Question 2 Media psychology (2)

(a) Outline the Hovland–Yale and Elaboration Likelihood models in explaining the persuasive effects of media.
(8 marks)

(b) Evaluate one of the models outlined in (a).
(16 marks)

ⓔ This is a question in parts. It asks for description in one part and evaluation in the other. Therefore, in part (a) only descriptive material must be offered relating to the two specified models. No marks are earned for including evaluative material.

In part (b) one of the theories only must be evaluated, though usage of the other theory could be creditworthy as long as it is used as a comparison. Purely descriptive material placed in this section will gain no credit.

Student answer

(a) The Hovland–Yale model **a** is centred on the role of persuasion, perceiving attitude change as a response to communication **c**. Less intelligent individuals are more easily persuadable, with self-esteem seen as an important factor, with individuals of moderate levels of intelligence more easily persuadable than those of high or low levels **c**. Mood is also an important factor **c**.

Target characteristics relate to the individual perceiving and processing a communication, while source characteristics **c** concern the credibility of the communicator **c**. More believable communicators are more persuasive, with credibility focused upon the skill and trustworthiness of a communicator and their level of attractiveness **c**.

Message characteristics concern the nature of a communication, with presentation of both sides of an argument seen as more persuasive towards attitude change **c**.

Overall the model sees attitude change as a process of stages, with the target person attending to a communication, comprehending it, reacting to it in a positive or negative fashion and finally accepting its credibility **c**.

The Elaboration Likelihood model **b** focuses on how persuasive messages are processed, perceiving two different forms of cognitive route by which persuasive attitude change can occur through cognitive evaluation **c**.

The central route occurs when individuals are presented with material and are motivated to analyse it carefully to reach an attitude-changing conclusion **c**. This route is important for messages requiring an elaborated cognitive effort, with such communications requiring robustness, as persuasion is influenced by the quality of the message **c**. If favourable thoughts are produced **c**, attitude change is likely.

The peripheral route occurs when individuals are motivated to consider the source of a communication to change attitudes, rather than the message itself **c**. Only superficial cues are considered **c**, like the perceived credibility of the communicator and the quality of the presentation, with the logic behind a message seen as irrelevant and requiring little or no elaboration.

> The central route c is likely to be used as motivation and the ability to process a message increases. Both central and peripheral routes c are used with situations of moderate elaboration.

e This part of the answer contains excellent outlines of the **a** Hovland–Yale and **b** Elaboration Likelihood models. **c** The material offered is relevant, clearly expressed and contains a wealth of detail. Indeed this is its shortcoming, as only 8 AO1 marks are available and the answer is far too long and thus takes away from valuable time better spent on the second part of the answer, where 16 marks are available.

> **(b)** The Elaboration Likelihood model is regarded as having explanatory power, but is lacking in predictive ability in the different contexts to which it can be applied **a**. The model attempts to address criticisms by continually updating and this is a good thing **a**.
>
> The sleeper effect **b** is a short-term effect, occurring when attitude changes are due to communicators being believable. However, this only occurs when a message is communicated to a person before they are told of its source and not the other way around.
>
> A negative aspect of the model is it describes the process of attitude change rather than actually explaining it **b**.
>
> Research tends to be laboratory based **c**, allowing causality to be established and permits replication to check the results, but this produces artificial findings due to the artificial environment in which experiments are carried out **a**.
>
> Research done into the role of fear in persuasive messages is potentially harmful **d** and therefore raises ethical issues that need to be attended to **a**.

e This part of the answer is too short for the 16 marks available for an evaluation and this has mostly occurred because too much time has been spent on the first part. Also the evaluative points made here often read like **a** a shopping list of points with no logical continuation between them and therefore no real elaboration and little effective commentary are evident. More importantly, some points raised relate to the **c** Hovland–Yale model and are therefore not creditworthy, as the question asked for only one of the theories outlined in part (a) to be evaluated. Relevant comments are made about **b** methodology and **d** ethics, but again these do not form part of an effective commentary.

(AO1 = 8/8) + (AO2/AO3 = 5/16) = 13/24 marks

Question 3 Media psychology (3)

Compare social psychological and evolutionary explanations for the attraction of celebrity.   (24 marks)

ⓔ This question focuses on two different explanations for the attraction of celebrity, with AO1 marks available for describing two explanations and AO2 marks available for an evaluation of them. The evaluation could focus on the degree of research support for the individual explanations, methodological concerns, practical applications and implications, as well as a direct comparison of the two explanations, drawing out their main strengths and weaknesses. It is also possible to include other explanations, but only if they are used as a part of the evaluation.

Student answer

There are a number of social psychological explanations, including social learning theory **a** which sees people observing and imitating celebrities in the media because they have qualities we admire. This therefore is a form of vicarious reinforcement **b**.

The absorption–addiction model **a** thinks celebrity interest comes from having no meaningful relationships, or wishing to escape a mundane existence. We're trying to develop a more positive self-image and feel more fulfilled.

Interest in celebrities is also explained by the positive-active model **a**, but for positive reasons, entailing active involvement like participating in fan clubs, which can increase social skills.

Evolutionary explanations **c** are different, seeing the attractiveness of celebrities as serving an adaptive function. The majority of evolution took place in the Pleistocene era, which ended about 10,000 years ago and therefore evolutionary-shaped behaviours are often addressed more to the environment of the past than the present. Any behaviour, such as celebrity worship, aiding survival will be acted upon by natural selection and become more prevalent in a population. Gossip about celebrities **d** may have evolved as a form of communicating social information within a group, such as about hierarchies. This can be seen in the modern day media, which churn out endless material on celebrities.

Dunbar (1997) thinks celebrity attraction is related to a need to prevent social free loading, where individuals receive more resources than they provide, suggesting an evolutionary explanation **f**.

Dunbar (1997) reports that 65% of conversation is social gossip, demonstrating that language may have evolved for social reasons **f**.

De Backer et al. (2005) found that interest in celebrity gossip fulfils the function of helping to acquire fitness-relevant survival information, supporting the idea of an evolved mechanism with an adaptive function **f**.

Fieldman (2008) found that females admire male celebrities demonstrating high levels of toughness, stamina and testosterone, as they're good advertisers of genetic quality, suggesting that celebrities are attractive for evolutionary reasons **f** related to sexual reproduction and mating strategies. This is backed up **f g** by Morin et al. (2008) finding that females are more influenced by celebrities endorsing products in advertisements, suggesting that celebrity attraction is part of the evolutionary idea of females being the selectors **f**.

One drawback with evolutionary theory **f** is that it can be seen as reductionist, reducing behaviour to the single explanation of adaptive fitness.

With social psychological explanations Chamberlain et al. (2009) found differences between the treatment of celebrities and non-celebrities, suggesting that celebrities receive more favourable treatment for social power and status reasons **e**.

Escalis and Bettman (2008) found support for the SLT, as celebrity endorsement enhances products due to people aspiring to be like celebrities **e**. They also found **g** that consumers build up connections to favourable celebrities and distance themselves from unfavourable ones, again supporting SLT **f**.

Derrick and Gabriel (2008) found that being attracted to celebrities is a good thing for those who experience difficulties with social relationships, because it improves self-esteem levels, bringing people closer to the ideals they hold about themselves. Crocker and Park (2004) support this **e g**, finding that those interested in celebrities are motivated to maintain and increase levels of self-esteem.

ⓔ The material on social psychological explanations is relevant and generally accurate. **a** Three explanations are offered here, the description of each being clear and coherent. However, the writing style of the student is not concise enough: more could be said in the same number of words. Each of these descriptions lacks detail, for instance **b** it is not made clear what 'vicarious reinforcement' is and so a deeper level of understanding is not conveyed to the examiner.

c The outline of evolutionary theory is accurate and again clearly expressed, but only a superficial link to the attraction of celebrity is given. One or two times 'celebrity' is mentioned, but with no real discussion of why the attractiveness of celebrities is explicable in evolutionary terms. **d** The final comment about gossip is relevant and the answer would benefit from more comments like this one.

The student chooses to evaluate the two explanations separately as **e** social explanations and **f** evolutionary explanations, which is fine, though a direct comparison would have allowed strengths and weaknesses to be better illustrated. All the material used is relevant and generally accurate.

There are a few instances where **g** material is built up to construct something resembling an effective commentary. More such instances are needed here to merit a higher mark.

(AO1 = 5/8) + (AO2/AO3 = 10/16) = 15/24 marks

Question 4 Psychology of addictive behaviour (1)

Discuss biological and cognitive approaches to explaining smoking and gambling.   (24 marks)

The instruction to 'discuss' involves descriptive and evaluative components. Material describing explanations for smoking and gambling addictions therefore earns AO1 credit, up to a maximum of 8 marks. Descriptions of research studies into smoking and gambling would be an effective way of gaining AO1 credit.

The evaluation part of the answer could be constructed in terms of research support, methodological and ethical considerations, practical applications as well as implications and contrasts with other explanations, as long as such material is used in an evaluative manner.

Student answer

Biological explanations of smoking **a** see nicotine **c** as affecting production of neurotransmitters like dopamine, producing a reinforcing effect. Variations in gene structure indicate individual differences in vulnerability, supporting **d** the biological explanation, for instance **d e** deCODE Genetics (2006) found genetic variations on chromosome 15 that elevate addiction risks, offering research support for the biological explanation as well as explaining **e** why some find it harder to quit. This is further supported by Pergadia (2006) finding a heritability factor in the experience of nicotine withdrawal symptoms, suggesting a genetic link **d e**. More support comes from Calvert (2009) finding the sight of cigarette packets caused activation in the ventral striatum and nucleus accumbens brain areas, again implying a biological explanation **d e**. This also suggests that anti-smoking adverts on cigarette packets won't persuade smokers to quit **e**. However, many quit without cravings, suggesting that social and cognitive factors play a role and addiction is mainly psychological **e**, as there seems to be little change in nicotine receptors that would characterise biological tolerance.

Biological explanations have been offered for gambling addiction **a**, with gambling **c** seen as affecting dopamine production, leading to pleasurable sensations in the brain reward system. Genetic factors **c** can explain why some are more at risk and some develop multiple addictions. Also gambling-orientated personalities **c** may be due to genetic factors. Roy (2004) offered support **d**, finding high levels of norepinephrine and dopamine levels in problem gamblers. This leads to heightened activation of the HPA axis and sympathoadrenergic system, suggesting that biological factors cause addiction. Grosset (2009) backed this up **d e**, finding that when dopamine agonists are used to treat Parkinson's disease, 10% of patients became problem gamblers. Further support came from Eisen (2001) **d e** who conducted twin studies to find a correlation between heredity and gambling as well as alcoholism, implying a biological explanation **e** for all addictions.

Cognitive explanations for smoking addiction **b** focus on the possession of irrational thoughts **c**, like 'smoking aids concentration'. This type of dysfunctional thinking can be self-fulfilling **c**, where not smoking is seen as causing concentration to wander, giving a strong reason not to quit. Similar distorted thought patterns **c** are used to explain gambling addiction too **b**, in that they distort beliefs about levels of

luck and skill, so successes are attributed to skill. Superstitious beliefs **c** therefore occur as ways of explaining successes and failures and the gambling becomes more problematic, with more risk taking and greater persistence.

Griffiths (1994) found that problem gamblers possess irrational views about losing, like it being due to not concentrating, and winning, such as it being due to personal skill, suggesting a cognitive explanation **d**. Further support **d e** came from Anholt (2003) finding that problem gamblers have obsessive–compulsive thoughts, suggesting **e** that dependency is explainable by cognitive factors.

Clark (2009) found gambling near misses were misperceived as special events, encouraging gambling to continue. Brain activity was heightened in the striatum and insula cortex, areas that receive input from dopamine and which have been linked to other forms of addiction, suggesting **d** cognitive distortions. Reinforcements and biological factors may all be involved in gambling dependency.

It is important that addictions are explained, as the consequences can be serious **f**.

Paul (2008) reports that 20% of teenage gambling addicts have contemplated suicide, demonstrating the need for valid explanations in order that effective treatments can be developed **f**.

(e) A reasonable attempt is apparent, which uses both **a** biological and **b** cognitive explanations to explain smoking and gambling addictions. Relevant, accurate and reasonably detailed material is evident, both in **c** descriptive and **d** evaluative passages, **e** with material often developed in a coherent fashion to form an effective commentary. Research material is especially well used, with clear explanations provided indicating a good level of understanding. Towards the end, **f** evaluative comments concerning implications/applications are also made. The material on biological explanations is made better use of, with the cognitive explanation possibly in need of a clearer explanation. Another way of improving this answer may have been to make reference to effective treatments based on the explanations, which would therefore offer support for the explanations.

(AO1 = 7/8) + (AO2/AO3 = 13/16) = 20/24 marks

Question 5 Psychology of addictive behaviour (2)

Outline and evaluate the role of media influences on addictive behaviour.   (24 marks)

ⓔ The outline for this question could focus on describing how different forms of media may affect addictive behaviour and the extent to which they have an effect, with an evaluation being built up around the extent to which research evidence supports this.

There are other aspects to explore too, like the effects of media demonisation of addicts and even the extent to which people can become addicts to media.

Student answer

A lot of research has been conducted into the effects media have on addictive behaviour **a**, enabling us to have a better understanding **b** of this important influence on dependency behaviours. Much of this research focuses on social learning effects **a**, for example Charlton (1986) found viewing cigarette advertisements made children associate smoking with looking grown up and having confidence, suggesting **b** that media influences lead to addiction **c**. However **g**, the media also have positive influences on addictive behaviours **d**, like the use of positive role models and education.

Gunsekera et al. (2005) found drug taking in films is shown in a positive fashion with little reference to possible negative consequences, suggesting **b** that the media can influence dependency behaviour in a negative manner **c**. However **g**, Roberts (2002) found contradictory evidence **b**, as drug taking in music videos was fairly uncommon **d**, portraying the behaviour in a neutral manner, though **g** this could actually increase drug usage by demonstrating it to be a normal behaviour **c**.

Although the media can help to inform about the risks of addiction **a**, there is a danger that addicts will be demonised through media-created moral panics **a**, seriously affecting the chances of addicts receiving enough social support to help them quit **b c**, or seeking treatment in the first place **b c**. Another danger **g** is that of misinformation **a**, with the National Pain Foundation (2008) **b** finding that the media confuse issues surrounding the addictive properties of painkilling drugs, leading to chronic undertreatment of pain **c**.

Another aspect is that of addiction to the media **a e**. Kimberley (2006) found social media to be extremely addictive **b**, leading to increased usage to sustain 'highs' and increased anxiety without regular access **c**. Relatively minor exposure was found to create dependence **c**, suggesting **b** social media addiction (SMA) to be a real and problematic disorder. Indeed **g** SMA is seen as such a problem that the Centre for Addiction Recovery has developed an internet addiction test **e** so people can see if they're at risk of developing the problem, demonstrating **b** how psychological methodology can be used in a practical way. Also **g** Walther (1999) **b** reported on the increase in communication addiction disorder (CAD) **e**, where the disinhibition of the internet makes it attractive to potential addicts who have problems in establishing and maintaining normal social relationships **c**. CAD creates serious disturbances in psychosocial functioning and an individual's ability to maintain positive work practices. This is backed up **b g** by Farber's (2007) research, finding SMA to be an increasing work problem, with many employees feeling a constant need to access social media sites to the point of dependency **c**, implying **b** that such behaviour can seriously affect performance and damage output.

Another consideration is people being affected differently by exposure to media sources a **f**, suggesting **b** there may be individual differences in vulnerability to addiction **f**, with this being linked to genetic factors **f**. Unlike the media portrayal **g**, addiction isn't a predictable side effect of narcotics, but may rather be a negative reaction by people with a genetic predisposition and psychological vulnerability to dependency.

Overall, the impact of media on addictive behaviour is hard to assess **b**, as research tends to display correlations, which don't display causality. Other variables may be involved too. However **g**, a consistent finding is media sources being influential with young children, as they don't question the credibility of media sources. It has been suggested **b** that there should be a ban on programmes with content concerning addictive behaviours until such children's bedtime.

e The student outlines a number of relevant points concerning **a** how the media influence addictive behaviour, **b** with evaluation of these points clearly signposted. A wide range of pertinent issues is covered, such as the **c** negative and **d** positive aspects of media coverage of addictive behaviours, **e** the problem of becoming addicted to media formats themselves **f** as well as possible differences in vulnerability levels.

Using this strategy it is fairly easy to construct an **g** effective, coherent and balanced commentary and this technique can be practised and improved by incorporating it into a regular revision strategy. Overall this answer has a reasonable outline that lacks some detail in its explanations, but has an effective, wide-ranging evaluation that places it in the top mark band.

(AO1 = 6/8) + (AO2/AO3 = 15/16) = 21/24 marks

Question 6 **Psychology of addictive behaviour (3)**

(a) Outline the theory of planned behaviour as a model for addiction prevention. (4 marks)

(b) Discuss the effectiveness of types of intervention used to reduce addictive behaviour. (20 marks)

ⓔ This is a question in parts that requires only descriptive material relating to the theory of planned behaviour as a model for addiction prevention in part (a). It should be noticed that part (a) offers 4 marks, so care should be taken not to overdo the description as it will not gain any extra credit and would waste valuable time better spent on part (b). It should also be remembered there are 4 more AO1 marks available in part (b) for outlining types of intervention, but that the vast majority of the marks available here is for an evaluation, which must focus on the effectiveness of the types of intervention outlined.

Student answer

(a) The theory of planned behaviour arose out of the earlier theory of reasoned action **a**, but with the addition of a new component, that of the influence of perceived control **a**. The model comprises several components **a**: behavioural beliefs, which determine one's attitude towards dependency **b**, normative beliefs, which concern social pressures to be involved in dependency behaviour **b** and control beliefs, which determine perceived behavioural control relating to an individual's belief that they can control their dependency behaviour **b**. If an individual's perceived behavioural control leads them to believe that they can control or quit their addiction **b** then the model predicts that they will be able to do so. Walsh and White (2007) found support for the theory **c**, as measurements of TPB constructs were found to accurately predict intentions and actual behaviour. This was further supported **c** by Oh and Hsu (2001), who found, using a questionnaire, an association between gamblers' attitudes, behavioural intentions and actual behaviour. However, a criticism of the model **c** is that it presumes behaviour is conscious, reasoned and planned, which may not necessarily always be the case with addicts and the model is also heavily reliant on evidence from self-reports, which may be subject to idealised answers **c** where addicts give responses according to how they'd like to be rather than how they actually are. In the model's favour, it does have a constructive practical application **c**, as a treatment process that health practitioners can tailor to individual addicts' needs.

ⓔ The first part of this answer **a** explains the TPB generally, **b** focusing specifically on addiction prevention as the question requires and in some detail, though not sufficiently to merit all 4 marks available. The second part of the answer goes on **c** to evaluate the theory, which is not required and which therefore is not creditworthy and wastes time that would have been better spent earning credit answering other questions.

AO1 = 3/4

(b) There are several types of intervention into addictive behaviours, such as biological ones like drug maintenance therapy **a**, involving the use of substitute drugs like methadone for heroin **b**. Less of a high is produced **b** and cues for addictive behaviour like spoons, silver foil and syringes aren't involved, as it's taken orally **b**. Another biological intervention is antagonistic and agonistic drugs **a**, with antagonistic ones being used to lessen the effects of neurotransmitters by blocking cellular activity and thus altering the addictive drug's effect **b**. Buprenorphine **b** is such a drug, used to treat morphine addiction. Agonistic drugs on the other hand trigger cellular activity by being site-specific **b**. Such a drug is Disulfiram **b**, used to combat cocaine addiction by heightening dopamine levels, lessening withdrawal symptoms and cravings by producing more dopamine in the brain.

There's research evidence indicating biological interventions to be effective against addictive behaviours **c**. Warren (2005) researched into the effectiveness of methadone as a treatment against heroin addiction among 900 prisoners. It was found that inmates using methadone used heroin on about 15 days a year, while inmates not receiving methadone used heroin on 100 days a year, suggesting that methadone is a very effective form of intervention **c**.

Psychological interventions, on the other hand, include aversion therapy, which is based on the behaviourist idea of classical conditioning, pairing an addictive substance with a negative effect so that they become associated together **d**.

SORRY, RAN OUT OF TIME.

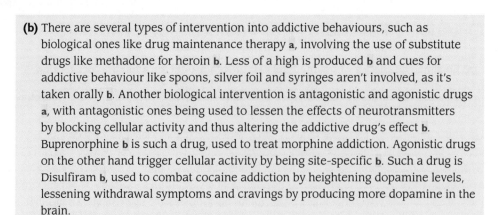 **a** Biological interventions are **b** outlined with accurate and relevant detail and **c** some effective evaluation based on research evidence is evident. The student then returns to **d** outlining a psychological intervention, but runs out of time, presumably having spent too long writing irrelevant evaluative material on the earlier part of this question. More than enough descriptive material has been given, though, to warrant awarding all 4 AO1 marks available.

(AO1 = 4/4) + (AO2/AO3 = 4/16) = 8/20

Question 7 **Anomalistic psychology (1)**

(a) Describe the Ganzfeld study method of ESP. (4 marks)

(b) Discuss the scientific status of parapsychology. (20 marks)

ⓔ This is a parted question, which requires only descriptive material relating to the Ganzfeld study method of ESP in part (a). It should be noticed that this is for 4 marks, so care should be taken not to overdo the description as it would not gain any extra credit and wastes valuable time better spent on part (b). It should also be remembered there are 4 more AOI marks available in part (b) for outlining issues of pseudoscience, but the vast majority of the marks, 16 of them, are available for an evaluation of the issues.

Student answer

(a) Ganzfeld literally means 'entire field' and was invented by Metzger in the 1930s as a means of researching Gestalt theory, which mainly relates to perception. It was Honorton (1974) who first used the technique as a means of investigating paranormal phenomena. Unpatterned sensory stimulation is used to produce a sensory deprivation effect, achieved by the receiver relaxing in a room with halved table-tennis balls over their eyes and headphones on playing white noise **a**. During this time the sender tries to communicate mentally a chosen target object **a**. Afterwards, in the judging phase, the receiver chooses one of four possible target images with a 25% possibility they'll get it right by chance **a**.

ⓔ **a** A relevant, focused, accurate and sufficiently detailed answer to be awarded the full 4 marks on offer. No evaluative content is given, which is good as no marks for an evaluation are awarded in this part of the question. This answer is about the right length for the hypothetical time allocation.

AOI = 4/4

(b) Sceptics accuse parapsychology of being pseudoscientific, a false science that lacks scientific rigour and practices **a**. The central problem is that science is based on sensory experience, while parapsychology is based on exchanges of information that go beyond sensory experience **a**. Therefore the fundamental argument is whether anomalistic phenomena are impossible by scientific definition, or whether science should not reject the possibility of such phenomena one day being shown to be true **a**. Another consideration here is that, when paranormal phenomena do become understood in a scientific manner, like hypnosis, then they're not considered paranormal anymore **a**.

Blackmore (2001) feels that the pseudoscience of parapsychology has become part of psychology because a belief exists that consciousness exists as a controlling mechanism of the mind, thus the desire to harness the 'power of consciousness' **b d**. However, this is just wishful thinking and has no basis in science **b**. Instead, as Sagan (2010) argues, parapsychology as a pseudoscience pretends to be scientific, but isn't based on scientific fact, ignores evidence that goes against it and is accepted too easily by a general public and some psychologists who wish it to be

true **b d**. Sagan sees the continuing popularity of parapsychology as due to its ability to fulfil strong emotional needs that science cannot satisfy, as well as satisfying the public's need for spiritual satisfaction, cures for disease and the existence of a comforting afterlife **b d**. Sceptics also see parapsychology as dressing itself up in scientific terminology and mirroring scientific practices in an attempt to be accepted as valid **b d**. However **b**, supporters **c** of the discipline argue that parapsychology has answered its critics by producing ever more stringent methodologies that exclude all human interference in research procedures so that no possibility of bias or fraud can exist and has continued to produce results beyond the boundaries of chance **b c**. In support of this view, Song (2006) argues that, if science automatically labels as pseudoscientific theories, like those found in parapsychology, which it doesn't understand, then science will be restrained from making innovative progress **b c**. Zhao doesn't agree with this **b d**, stating instead that science isn't over-conservative and does accept revolutionary ideas if they're supported by persuasive evidence.

It is important that parapsychological phenomena are not accepted as true without convincing evidence **b**, as their acceptance could lead to dangerous and inefficient practical applications **d**, such as the acceptance of invalid therapies as being beneficial.

Perhaps the fundamental problem with parapsychological phenomena **b** is reflected in the fact that supporters tend to find evidence of their existence, while sceptics cannot replicate these findings. This suggests that biased, wishful thinking may be occurring on one or even both sides of the argument.

@ An excellent answer. **a** A concise, relevant and detailed outline of the debate is given that is easily worth the 4 marks on offer. The evaluation that then follows is **b** built from a series of well connected theoretical viewpoints that gives a balanced argument, considering both arguments **c** for and **d** against parapsychology being a scientific discipline. This builds into a coherent, elaborated and effective commentary and scores at the highest level possible.

(AOI = 4/4) + (AO2/AO3 = 16/16) = 20/20

Question 8 Anomalistic psychology (2)

Outline and evaluate explanations for superstitious behaviour and magical thinking.   (24 marks)

ⓔ This is a straightforward essay question that requires a description of explanations for superstitious behaviour and magical thinking in order to gain the 8 AO1 marks on offer. The remaining 16 marks are available for an evaluation of these factors, which would probably be most focused upon the degree of research support there is for the explanations, though material could also be offered, if made relevant, on practical applications and methodological considerations.

People tend to believe in superstitions, as they have a desire for control and certainty **a**. A superstition therefore gives a sense of understanding phenomena, like what is needed to achieve success **a**, as well as a means of achieving this, like wearing your lucky jumper **a**. Superstitions are also explicable through behaviourism via operant conditioning **a**. This can be either through positive reinforcement where a certain behaviour or object becomes associated with a desirable outcome **a**, like your lucky jumper becoming associated with your football team winning, or through negative reinforcement, where a behaviour or object becomes associated with reducing the anxiety associated with uncertainty **a**, such as being anxious about the performance of your football team and believing that wearing your lucky jumper gives you some control over the outcome of a game.

Magical thinking can be explained through the law of similarity, where similar events and objects are seen as connected in some psychic way **b**, like the same things happening to twins in different places, as well as the law of contagion, where things that have been associated with each other retain paranormal connections when separate **b**, like dead saints' bones having healing powers.

Skinner (1948) **e** found that pigeons developed superstitions based on unique body movements through associating such movements with being rewarded with food pellets, which supports **c** the behaviourist explanation. The idea that superstitious behaviour is connected to a desire for control and certainty is also supported **c**, as Fluke (2010) **e** found three reasons for superstitious beliefs: to gain control over uncertainties, to decrease feelings of helplessness and because it's easier to rely on superstitions than coping strategies. This research therefore additionally suggests **c** that superstitions can be positive, a point backed up **c** by Lustberg (2004) **e**, who found that superstitions among sportsfolk were beneficial, as they increased confidence, motivation and persistence, which increased chances of winning. Therefore, although superstitions are irrational, having no basis in fact, they can be psychologically healthy **c** by reducing anxiety levels and increasing self-assurance. Kienan (1994) **e**, though, points out that they can also be psychologically unhealthy **c**. He found that Israelis with the highest stress levels after Iraqi missile attacks had the greatest beliefs in superstitions, which suggests **c** that superstitions create an illusion in the possessor that they have control over outcomes and therefore are responsible for missiles hitting targets and killing people. This creates anxiety. Some superstitions actually aren't irrational **f**, but have a basis in fact, such as spilling salt being unlucky. Salt was a valuable commodity necessary for survival, therefore

losing it could lead to death. This suggests **c** that some superstitions have an educational value to them that aids survival.

Magical thinking is also supported **d**, such as Lawrence (1994) finding that childhood traumas and a belief in magical thinking are correlated, which suggests that magical thinking acts as a coping strategy in those who've suffered trauma **d**.

e The answer outlines explanations for both **a** superstitious behaviour and **b** magical thinking in a relevant and accurate manner, though a little more detail would have been desirable. The evaluation is unbalanced, as it is mainly centred on **c** superstition rather than **d** magical thinking. The evaluation of superstition is done well, **e** using several pieces of research evidence to build an effective, elaborated commentary. Some creditworthy contrasting points are also made, **f** such as superstitions being sometimes based on fact. Overall a reasonable answer that would have benefited from more evaluation of magical thinking.

(AO1 = 6/8) + (AO2/AO3 = 11/16) = 17/24

Question 9 Anomalistic psychology (3)

Discuss psychological research into ONE of the following:
- **psychic healing**
- **out-of-body and near-death experience**
- **psychic mediumship**   (24 marks)

ⓔ The question offers a choice here, so only one of the offered options must be chosen. If more than one was chosen, all would be marked but only the best one credited. The injunction to discuss incorporates both the need to describe the chosen option and to evaluate it. It should be remembered that the term research includes both research studies and explanations/theories.

Student answer

Psychic healing **a** is a well documented, long-occurring phenomenon, where people have apparent healing powers, usually by a laying on of hands or use of crystals to tap into energy fields, but healing can also occur over large distances with no physical contact. Such a 'gift' is often in the possession of charismatic, religious-type figures **a** and psychologists have conducted research **a** to try to see if the phenomenon is genuine or faked. Grad (1959) **b** studied a man who discovered a healing gift while tending to horses. It was found during treatments by him that production of an enzyme was stimulated and Krieger (1979) **b** studying the same man, found elevated haemoglobin, suggesting **c** a biological basis to his powers. However, Ostrander (1970) **b** studied another apparent healer who placed his hands near, but not on patients' bodies, who reported a sensation of heat, finding no changes in temperature occurring, implying **c** any beneficial effects to be the result of suggestion rather than a real biological occurrence.

One thing that should be considered is that doctors are trained how to cure people, but few psychic healers have such training, therefore how can psychics treat people without having any medical knowledge or training, unless they're tapping into natural bodily defences **c**?

West (1957) **b** reviewed medical records of 11 miracle cures of people visiting Lourdes, finding that crucial information necessary to assess such claims was missing. As lots of sick people have visited the shrine at Lourdes, it's quite possible such 'miracles' occurred quite by chance **c**. The Catholic Church, after reviewing scientific literature, even decided to ban the use of therapeutic touch as a valid form of treatment **c**.

Braud and Schlitz (1988) **b** looked into distance learning, getting psychic healers to focus on a photo of a patient without the patient being aware of this, ruling out any possibility of a placebo effect occurring **c**. It was found that galvanic skin responses, associated with the sympathetic nervous system were altered, indicating a real, biological factor at play **c**.

It may well be that research into this area, especially in the past, hasn't been conducted under stringent enough conditions, allowing experimenter effects and demand characteristics to occur **c**. It may now not be possible to replicate old studies **c**, so new ones will have to be performed. Also many gullible people might be paying out loads to false healers **c** and this gives them elevated respectability and status, leading to even more people trusting and paying them **c**.

A possible benefit of psychic healing **c d** is pointed out by Mollica (2005) **a**, who suggests that such psychics could help treat the trauma that occurs during environmental catastrophes like an earthquake. If they are treating patients who are used to such methods as part of their culture, then they'll probably be more effective at reducing trauma **c d** than unaccustomed medical practices, which might actually raise anxiety **c** and be very intrusive **c**.

It seems overall **e** that psychic healing may have a real medical biological effect **c**, but then again it could just be a form of spontaneous recovery **c**, occurring due to the presence of a caring person who reduces fears and worries, assisting recovery from illness. Also it could just be a short-term recovery followed by relapse, occurring due to the power of suggestion **c**. The placebo effect could be occurring too **c**, where a false treatment works as the patient believes it and therefore has the expectation it will be of benefit.

e This answer **a** begins with a general description of psychic healing, before **b** outlining relevant research studies, which are accurate, though at times lacking in the detail required to convey total understanding of the topic. **c** A number of coherent evaluative points are made, though these can be somewhat disjointed and therefore don't really form an effective commentary. This is probably the result of planning out the answer poorly. Taking a little time before writing an essay to construct a plan of linked points can often be beneficial. Also included are **d** some indications of the implications of psychic healing, with **e** the final paragraph serving as a kind of conclusion, but lacking effectiveness, as much of it repeats material already covered.

(AOI = 7/8) + (AO2/AO3 = 12/16) = 19/24 marks

Question 10 Psychological research and scientific method

ⓔ With the research methods question, care should be taken to answer the actual questions being asked and not to wander off the point and include irrelevant material. It is also important to use the mark allocations as a rough guide as to how much material is needed to gain all the marks available.

Note: for reasons of clarity and accessibility answers to this question have been included after each part of the question.

A team of researchers wanted to see if animals distribute themselves at different sites within an environment according to the availability of food.

Using a local duck pond, a field experiment was conducted where one researcher threw bread pellets into the pond every 5 seconds at feeding site (A), while a second researcher threw identically-sized bread pellets into the pond every 10 seconds at feeding site (B). A third researcher recorded the number of ducks at both sites every 30 seconds for 5 minutes.

After 5 minutes the feeding rates were swapped, with bread pellets being thrown in the pond every 10 seconds at feeding site (A) and every 5 seconds at feeding site (B). The third researcher again recorded the number of ducks at both sites for another 5 minutes, so that in all 20 pieces of data were collected from each feeding site.

The table below shows a summary of the results.

Total and mean number of ducks present at 5- and 10-second feeding site schedules

	Feeding site (A)	Feeding site (B)
Total number of ducks present during 5-second feeding schedule	184	190
Mean number of ducks present during 5-second feeding schedule	18.4	19.0
Total number of ducks present during 10-second feeding schedule	122	124
Total number of ducks present during 10-second feeding schedule	12.2	12.4

(a) Identify the type of design used in the study.   (1 mark)

(a) A repeated measures design has been used.

(b) Identify one extraneous variable that might occur and explain how this could be dealt with.   (4 marks)

(b) The ducks might not be able to see both feeding sites and therefore do not really have a choice. This could be addressed by putting the sites close enough together to allow the ducks to see and have a choice, but not too close together so that we couldn't see which site they were at.

(c) Name an appropriate statistical test for analysing the data. Explain why this would be a suitable test to use. (4 marks)

(c) Wilcoxon matched-pairs, signed-ranks is suitable, as it's a test of difference, can be used with a repeated measures design and requires data to be at least ordinal level.

(d) Explain what is meant by the results being found to be significant at the 5% level of significance. (2 marks)

(d) This means that the results are accepted as showing a real difference beyond the boundaries of chance, with a 5% possibility that they actually occurred by chance.

(e) Give one reason why the researchers used a one-tailed test. (2 marks)

(e) A one-tailed hypothesis has been used, as previous research indicates the direction the results should go in.

(f) With reference to the data in the table, outline and discuss the findings of this investigation. (10 marks)

(f) There are more ducks at the faster feeding sites. When site (A) was the 5-second schedule feeding site there was a mean of 18.4 ducks and similarly a mean of 19.0 when site (B) was the faster feeding site, compared with a mean of only 12.2 for site (A) when it was the slower 10-second schedule feeding site and 12.4 for feeding site (B). This shows that it's not a particular site that is preferred but the feeding rate itself, as the ducks are re-allocating themselves when the feeding rate changes and the overall mean feeding rate for each site, taking into account the 5- and 10-second schedules, is very similar at 15.3 ducks for site (A) and 15.7 ducks for site (B). This is only possible to see because the order of presentation of the feeding sites has been counterbalanced to address any possible order effects.

The use of the mean as a measure of central tendency gives us a representative average score, as it takes into account all the scores, though the weakness of the mean is that it can be skewed by 'rogue' extreme outlying values.

There is a total of 374 ducks at the faster feeding sites, compared with only 246 at the slower sites and what this tells us, apart from confirming the faster 5-second

AQA(A) A2 Psychology

site as more popular, is that about two-thirds of the ducks are at the faster feeding rate site and one-third at the slower feeding rate site. This suggests that the ducks are allocating themselves at a ratio where they would have access to the optimal amount of food available.

(g) The researchers noted that the older-looking ducks seemed to distribute themselves more quickly than did the younger-looking ducks. Design a study to investigate the relationship between age and speed of distribution. You should include sufficient details to permit replication, for example a hypothesis, variables, details of design and procedure, sampling.

(12 marks)

(g) A correlational study would need to be conducted, where one co-variable would be the age of the ducks in years and the second co-variable would be how fast they distributed themselves to a feeding site, measured in seconds. A one-tailed directional hypothesis would be that there will be a significant positive relationship between the age of ducks in years and how quickly they distribute themselves to feeding sites.

A stratified sample would need to be used so that there was an equal number of ducks of various ages and these would need to be marked in some way to identify what age they were.

Model answers are evident throughout the answer, with all information offered being geared towards the questions. Sufficient accurate elaboration is provided to justify full marks being awarded for all parts.

(AO1 = 3/3) + (AO2 = 4/4) + (AO3 = 28/28) = 35/35 marks

Knowledge check answers

1 Media can influence pro- and antisocial behaviour through *social learning*, where behaviour in others is observed and imitated, with viewers learning how and when to imitate behaviour according to how it is reinforced, especially if they identify with the model. *Cognitive priming* is another media influence where pro- and antisocial behaviours witnessed are stored to be 'triggered' into action by similar scenarios. *Stereotyping* exaggerates and communicates models of pro- and antisocial behaviour in an easily understandable way that makes their imitation easier. *Desensitisation* mainly affects antisocial behaviour, making it less objectionable by reducing cognitive, emotional and behavioural responses to it. *Displacement* occurs by the media amplifying antisocial behaviour to make the world seem more dangerous than it is.

2 Video games reinforce behaviours by rewarding them within games. Frequent players can become retarded in emotional regulation skills by becoming desensitised to cues that trigger empathetic responses, making acceptance of antisocial behaviour likelier. Repeated exposure to violence can also lead to desensitisation, with similar effects. Games can, however, have a positive influence on self-esteem and confidence levels and be a source of catharsis, where aggression is released in a non-harmful manner. Computers can lead to deindividuation, where individuals lose the normal checks on their behaviour, which leads to disinhibition and antisocial behaviour. Computers can also be a positive tool for communicating, learning and developing social skills.

3 The Hovland–Yale model centres on the role of persuasion in bringing about attitude change through several factors. First, *target characteristics* concerning personality features of individuals receiving communications, such as their levels of intelligence and self-esteem. Second, *source characteristics* concerning how credible communicators are in terms of expertise, trustworthiness and attractiveness, and, third, *message characteristics* concerning the nature of a communication, with balanced messages seen as more persuasive.

4 The Elaboration Likelihood model focuses on the cognitive routes through which persuasive attitude change occurs by cognitive evaluation. First, the *central route*, by cognitive evaluation of important messages, with attitude change occurring if the quality of a message is high. Second, the *peripheral route*, where the source of a message rather than the message itself is considered, such as the credibility of the communicator. This occurs for less important messages.

5 The Hovland–Yale model uses three factors to explain the persuasiveness of television advertising: (i) the *communicator*, with skilled, attractive and trustworthy communicators seen as more persuasive; (ii) the *message*, where the immediacy and wide availability of television are seen as persuasive for simple messages; (iii) the *audience*, with females more persuadable by male-based topics and males more by female-based topics, with age-related differences also existing.

The Elaboration-Likelihood model explains the persuasiveness of television advertising as more effective through the central route, if messages are important to an audience and robust enough to withstand elaborated cognitive effort. The peripheral route also plays a role in making less important messages persuasive, for instance in maintaining positive emotional states. The model also sees a big role for heightened emotions in capturing an audience's attention.

6 SLT sees celebrities as desirable models to observe and imitate to gain the reinforcements their fame is perceived as bringing them. SIT sees an individual's social identity as influenced through membership of in-groups, created by groups of celebrity admirers coming together. Social construction theory perceives celebrity as a social invention of the media to generate income. The absorption–addiction model sees individuals who lack meaningful relationships and lifestyles as trying to gain more self-esteem by attraction to celebrity, which can become addictive and harmful to psychological health. The positive-active model sees celebrity interest as more healthy, through development of social skills.

7 Evolutionary explanations see attraction to celebrity as having a survival value through its adaptive function. Celebrities themselves have an adaptive advantage with their increased access to resources through their attractiveness, while celebrity gossip permits communication of useful information about alpha males and females. Female focus on male celebrities allows them to learn about desirable qualities in males, useful for mate selection purposes, and on female celebrities to learn attractiveness skills, as well as competing in levels of attractiveness. The prestige hypothesis sees imitation of celebrities as beneficial in bringing the same increased resources to which celebrities have access.

8 Intense fandom can be healthy for individuals of low self-esteem who are interested in celebrities for their entertainment value, as research suggests they assimilate celebrities' characteristics, thus boosting their self-esteem. More intense versions of fandom can be unhealthy, leading to eating disorders and obsessional behaviour that is borderline pathological.

9 Research suggests that celebrity stalkers are different from other varieties of stalker, with celebrity stalkers tending to have insecure attachment types and positive attitudes towards obsessional behaviours. Kamphuis and Emmelkamp (2000) categorised different types of stalker, perceiving celebrity stalkers as psychotic, characterised by impulsive, antisocial, egocentric behaviour.

10 The biological model sees addiction as physiologically controlled, with initiation occurring through a combination of genetic vulnerability and environmental triggers. Maintenance occurs through the pleasurable production of dopamine, with relapses occurring due to physiological cravings. With smoking, nicotine is physically addictive and both smoking and gambling affect neurotransmitter levels, such as dopamine and acetylcholine, to produce pleasurable effects, with genetics determining individual levels of vulnerability.

11 The cognitive model sees addiction as occurring through distorted thinking related to dysfunctional beliefs about dependency behaviours. Addicts often believe they cannot control their behaviour, and maintenance and relapse also occur through irrational focus on positive effects, often short-term pleasurable ones, rather than negative, long-term ones. Smokers and gamblers often have an irrational belief that they cannot quit, with smokers focusing on supposed positive effects, such as smoking improving concentration, while gamblers hold irrational beliefs about skill and luck levels, which lead to maintenance of gambling dependency and greater risk-taking.

12 The learning model explains addiction as occurring through classical conditioning, where dependency behaviours become associated with particular environmental features (e.g. gambling when in a betting shop), and operant conditioning through positive reinforcements (e.g. smoking highs), and negative reinforcements (e.g. the easing of cravings). SLT sees dependency as occurring via observation and imitation of models demonstrating dependency behaviours and seen to be reinforced for doing so. With smoking, nicotine is positively and negatively reinforcing, while gambling can be explained in terms of classical and operant conditioning, as well as SLT.

13 Social stressors such as poverty are linked to increased vulnerability to addiction, with those who are more sensitive to the effects of stress most vulnerable. There is also increased stress from trying to quit and maintaining quitting, making relapse more likely.

Peers are especially influential in initiating and maintaining dependency behaviours through conformity, operant conditioning and SLT.

With age, adolescence is a prime time for initiation and, the earlier dependency behaviours start, the harder it is to quit, with an increased chance of developing multiple addictions. Old age is also seen as a gateway to increased vulnerability to addiction.

With personality, neurotic and psychopathic types are more vulnerable to addiction, in order to try to reduce the effects of stressors that don't affect other personality types so much.

14 Media can influence addictive behaviour through social learning, and by presenting enhanced opportunities for observation and imitation of models seen to be reinforced for their behaviour. Addiction to media itself is becoming an increasing problem, as more and more people become dependent on technology. Media can also affect people's perceptions of vulnerability to addiction by misrepresenting addiction risks.

15 TPB as a model of addiction prevention takes into account reasons for maintenance of dependency behaviours and individual resolve to quit, and revolves around control beliefs, involving the perceived presence of factors seen as helping or hindering attempts to quit. Abstention is seen as being dependent on perceived behavioural control being focused on the belief that an individual has the capability to quit. The higher this is, the higher the chances of abstention, and attempts to quit will be greater the more difficult abstention is perceived to be.

16 Biological interventions involve physical detoxification and drug maintenance therapy, involving less addictive antagonistic and agonistic drugs to reduce dependency. Biological interventions are effective but only in treating physical symptoms and not in addressing psychological reasons for dependency, and can incur harmful side effects.

Cognitive interventions seek to replace irrational thought processes with rational ones, with therapies like CBT helping to reduce cravings and develop the willpower to abstain. Research suggests CBT can be highly effective.

Interventions based on behaviourism use classical and operant conditioning to replace maladaptive dependency behaviours with adaptive non-dependent ones. Behavioural interventions can work in the short term but do not address underlying reasons for addiction, so dependency may return.

Public health interventions use legislation and fear arousal, and give advice and target at-risk groups to try to reduce dependency behaviours. All can be effective, but especially when targeted at groups identified as at risk of dependency.

17 Parapsychology has tried to establish itself as science by adopting rigorous scientific methods. Some paranormal phenomena, like hypnosis, are now understood from a scientific viewpoint. Sceptics argue that other paranormal phenomena are scientifically impossible, while others believe that the possibility of such phenomena cannot be rejected.

18 There is research evidence both to support and not support the existence of ESP through the Ganzfeld technique. Experimental techniques have become progressively stricter and more rigorous, with computer-controlled tests, randomisation of targets and electromagnetically shielded testing rooms to avoid human interference. The central finding is that, when sceptics perform research, non-significant results are found, while believers find significant results.

19 As with ESP, there is evidence both to support and refute the existence of PK. Again, positive results seem mainly to come from believers in the phenomenon and independent researchers generally cannot replicate such findings. The magician James Randi has demonstrated fraudulent ways of achieving positive results and asks the question that, if PK does exist, why don't its practitioners use it for human good?

20 Coincidences and probability judgements are miscalculated when people overemphasise examples of coincidences as being the norm. This can occur due to errors in memory but happens mainly when people fail to use logical reasoning and create a cognitive bias due to (i) having an intuitive thinking style that lacks critical thinking; (ii) forming cognitive illusions, where significance is read into random patterns; (iii) an illusion of control, where random processes are seen as under personal control; and (iv) a confirmatory bias, where contrary evidence is ignored.

21 Superstitions occur due to a desire for certainty and control, which involves searching for rules for why things occur as they do, so that desirable outcomes can be produced. Behaviourism sees superstitions as occurring due to reinforcements, where behaviours become associated with pleasurable outcomes or

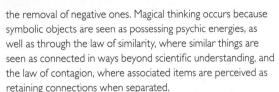

the removal of negative ones. Magical thinking occurs because symbolic objects are seen as possessing psychic energies, as well as through the law of similarity, where similar things are seen as connected in ways beyond scientific understanding, and the law of contagion, where associated items are perceived as retaining connections when separated.

22 Neuroticism is associated with paranormal belief as it is a source of comfort that lessens the effects of negative emotions. Extroverts are more likely to have ESP abilities, while defensive individuals, who cognitively resist threatening situations/information, have poor ESP abilities. Superstitious individuals have an external locus of control linked to a belief in fate, while believers in ESP have an internal locus of control related to a belief in control through willpower.

23 Psychic healing involves healing people, often by charismatic individuals, in ways not understood scientifically, which involves physical or non-physical contact, sometimes over long distances. Sometimes a healing medium is used, such as crystals, to achieve the effect. Recovery may be due to real biological effects or spontaneous recovery similar to a placebo effect.

24 NDEs are linked with OBEs, as they often involve OBEs too. OBEs involve individuals experiencing feeling external to their body, either (i) parasomatic (having a body other than their own) or (ii) asomatic (having no body). OBEs are linked to sleep and dream states, as they often occur in bed or when taking drugs that induce dream states, possibly because dream images mix with usual sensory input.

25 Psychic mediums claim to be able to communicate with the spirit world in various ways, often to help individuals contact significant others who have died. Physical mediums permit contact through viewable, physical means, such as the manifestation of voices and visible figures, while mental mediums permit contact through non-viewable, non-physical means, such as: clairvoyance, where a medium sees spirits; clairaudience, where a medium hears spirits; clairsentience, where a medium senses thoughts and emotions of spirits; and trance mediumship, where spirits speak through a medium. Other sensory stimuli may simultaneously occur too, such as aromas, tactile experiences and changes in temperature.

26 Science involves: replicability, where research is repeated to check the results; objectivity, where research must be conducted without bias; falsification, where theories are constructed that are capable of being proven wrong; hypothesis testing, where predictions are generated from observations and rigorously tested; and the use of empiricism, where observations are based upon sensory experience rather than on thoughts and beliefs.

27 Peer review may be biased by researchers' social relationships and rivalries with each other and by organisations that fund research having financial interest in certain research being accepted as scientifically valid. There may also be resistance to accepting groundbreaking research, especially as peer review tends to be dominated by elites from the mainstream of science. The work of well known researchers may also be preferred over that of new researchers.

28 (a) Although random sampling involves unbiased selection, it does not necessarily produce representative samples, as all of one kind of participant might be selected, e.g. all females. (b) Systematic sampling and stratified sampling produce fairly representative samples.

29 Ethical guidelines were introduced to ensure that the safety and dignity of participants were not compromised. Previous research had attracted criticisms that participants had been misled and subjected to harm. Without the support and confidence of the public, psychology cannot function as a meaningful scientific discipline.

30 The concept of probability involves ascertaining whether differences and relationships found in research are meaningful and significant beyond the boundaries of chance. A significance level represents the cut-off point beyond which results are seen as meaningful and not due to chance factors.

31 The three factors that need to be considered when selecting a statistical test are whether a difference or a relationship is being tested for, what level of data has been measured (nominal, ordinal or interval) and, with experiments, what design has been used (IGD, RMD or MPD).

32 Psychological investigations are written in a conventional manner to permit replication. Science requires that all results can be authenticated and shown to be valid, therefore research is written up in a manner that permits exact replication to occur, so that such authentication purposes can be realised.

AQA(A) A2 Psychology